CUPCAKES & PARTIES!

Mangez Bien
Riez Souvent
Aimez Beaucoup
epoisses berthaut
pain au levain
baguettes
legumes

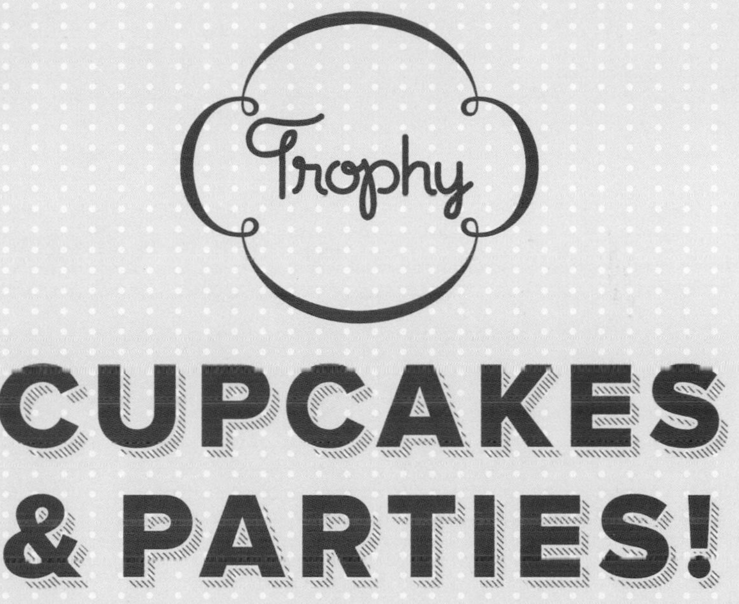

CUPCAKES & PARTIES!

Deliciously Fun Party Ideas and Recipes from Seattle's Prize-Winning Cupcake Bakery

JENNIFER SHEA

PHOTOGRAPHS *by* RINA JORDAN

SASQUATCH BOOKS
SEATTLE

I proudly dedicate this book to my mom for teaching me to craft and bake . . . and pay attention to all of the little details.

And to Michael and Fleetwood for making every day feel like a magical party.

Printed in China
Published by Sasquatch Books
17 16 15 14 9 8 7 6 5 4 3

Editor: Susan Roxborough
Project editor: Nancy W. Cortelyou
Design: Anna Goldstein
Photographs: Rina Jordan
Prop styling: Jenn Elliott Blake
Craft creator: Jenny Batt
Illustrations: Julia Manchik
Copy editor: Diane Sepanski

Library of Congress Cataloging-in-Publication
Data is available.

ISBN: 978-1-57061-864-2

Sasquatch Books
1904 Third Avenue, Suite 710
Seattle, WA 98101
(206) 467-4300
www.sasquatchbooks.com
custserv@sasquatchbooks.com

CONTENTS

Happy Birthday
HAPPY HOME

CUPCAKES

Trophy
Trophy
Trophy
Trophy
Trophy
Trophy
Trophy
Trophy
Trophy
Trophy
Trophy

THE PARTY STARTS HERE

Why I'm obsessed with creating joyful celebrations.

You could say that party planning is in my DNA. I'm not sure which of my ancestors was first bit by the hospitality bug, but I clearly come from a family of celebrators with a flair for festivities and a knack for fun. Take my first birthday party. My mom marked the anniversary of my first twelve months with a Raggedy Ann theme, complete with a rag doll shaped sheet cake and copious decorations, favors, and games in red, white, and gingham blue—let's just say that shades of Miss Ann were found in just about every corner of our house that day. Looking back, I'm surprised Mom didn't dress me in candy-cane tights and tie a wig of dyed mop yarn on my head! Her father, my grandfather, was also a legendary host, often throwing cocktail parties where everyone dressed to the nines and danced through the night, while *his* parents, my great-grandparents, once celebrated Halloween (this was long before grown-ups were crazy for Halloween parties) with an elaborate costume gala that my relatives still talk about to this day.

So as you can imagine, I was hooked on entertaining from the start. I began crafting and baking (mostly fresh blackberry pies!) with my mom when I was knee high, and I won a couple of baking contests including a blue ribbon for my grandma's Pumpkin Roll by the time I was eight, as well as the Home Economics Award in the 8th grade. Pretty soon, I was the unofficial family baker and party-maker, frequently enlisted to make cakes for parties and generally depended on to deliver magic through vanilla and buttercream. I loved the challenge and the pleasure that comes from feeding others with beautiful, sweet confections. Through the years I never stopped baking and always gravitated toward entertaining and food, whether working in bakeries and restaurants or earning my bachelor of science in nutrition (yes, this cupcake lady has a degree in nutrition!).

At Trophy, we believe every day should be a party—filled with colorful confetti, exquisite treats, and happy surprises. We are confection creators, fun curators, and magicians of *mmmmm*. And every day, we pour our hearts into inspiring truly amazing parties.

Trophy was founded in 2007 by dessert lover Jennifer Shea and her husband Michael Williamson. Jennifer's passion for dreamy, decadent desserts has made Trophy Seattle's favorite boutique cupcake bakery. Even Martha Stewart calls Jennifer's cupcakes "utterly delicious!" They adore serving up party-perfect confections and accoutrements from their five Seattle-area locations—and are thrilled to share their love of all things fun and scrumptious in this book.

As you can see, it was no great surprise when some years later my husband Michael and I opened a cupcake and party store and pretty much made it our life's work to "make every day a party." The first Trophy Cupcakes and Party opened in a cinnamon-colored historic schoolhouse in 2007 after eight years of recipe testing. Our plan? Make delicious, magical, and transcendent cupcakes in a festive space that would inspire others to celebrate the good things in life—and do it often.

My inspiration for Trophy came from any number of the gazillion European bakeries I visited while traveling over the years. Stop in just about any town in France and Italy, and you'll find a shop that sells bread, another that sells cake, and still another that sells candies. I became obsessed with the idea of putting all my heart into just one craft and making it the best it could be. Cupcakes became my mantra, and my motivation came through the joy of upholding the age-old tradition of artisan-style baking.

I learned early on that the best ingredients make the biggest smiles. So at Trophy, we only use pure cane sugar; local, hormone-free dairy products and eggs; French cocoa; Belgian chocolate; pure Madagascar Bourbon vanilla; organic berries—you get the idea (see Use Trophy-Worthy Ingredients, page 26). I will never bend or compromise on ingredients! And it sounds clichéd, but love and care *must* go into every cupcake to bring out the magic. I always say, if you're going to indulge, it should be on the very *best*.

CUPCAKES
Trophy
AND PARTY

Trophy Cupcakes
are baked from scratch
throughout the day using th
finest quality ingredients.
Details like Valrhona coco
local sweet cream butter an
dairy products (rBGH-free) p
Madagascar Bourbon vani
free-range eggs, Callebau
chocolate, organic peanut
butter and fresh fruit make
party-perfect little cakes
something to celebrate!

I Believe in You
THANK YOU SO VERY MUCH FOR YOUR KINDNESS
YOU ARE TOTALLY THE BEE'S KNEES
LOVE IT!
LET'S MAKE OUT
CONGRATULATIONS
FOR THE BRIDE AND GROOM
Congratulations

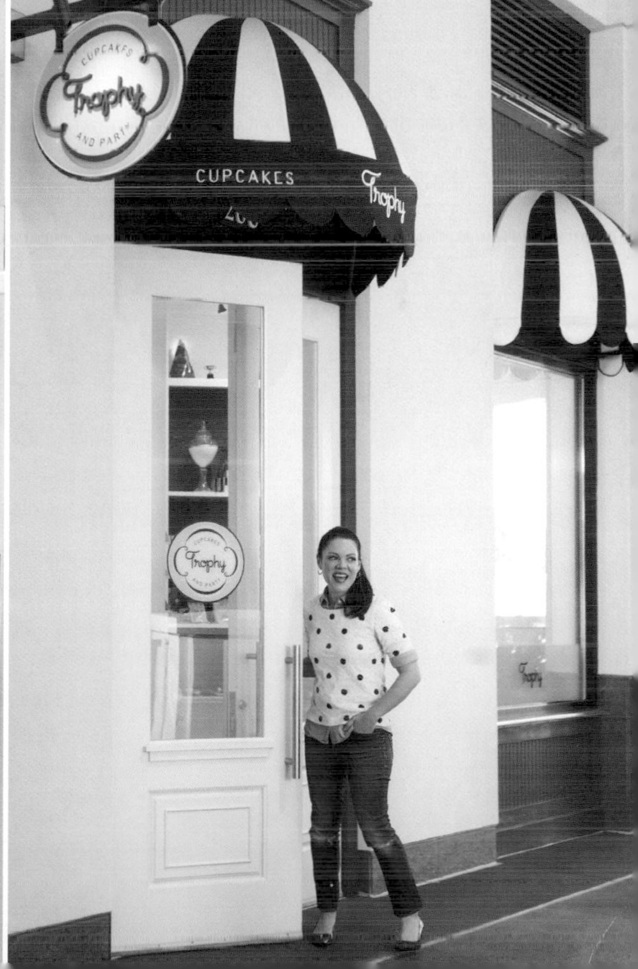
CUPCAKES
Trophy
AND PARTY
CUPCAKES
Trophy

PRO-TIP

Scan and print worksheets and other resources straight from this book, or visit the Printables section of our website at TrophyCupcakes.com/book, to download all of my best party-planning tools.

Trophy's look and style are inspired solely and simply by things Michael and I love. Our striped awnings are an homage to European bakeries; hand-painted signs recall old-world specialty shops; our marble countertops are like ones I've seen in 1940s bakery photos; and the aqua decor matches my collection of vintage Franciscan dishes. Historically, cake is equated with celebrations, so I created an area in our stores displaying a handpicked selection of truly festive items, such as nostalgia-inspired party favors, so that people can take the magic home with them.

But it wasn't until after I planned my son Fleetwood's first birthday party (a playful circus theme in red, white, and blue—Mom clearly hard-wired that color story into my consciousness early on!) that I realized not everyone has the gene for throwing magical parties. By his second and third birthdays (with French Nautical and Woodland Creatures themes, respectively), I'd overheard other moms whispering that they "could never do anything like this" and "wouldn't know where to start." It hadn't occurred to me that throwing a party isn't as simple as having the tools, such as pretty decorations and yummy sweets. No, a memorable party comes from an inspired idea—and a well-organized checklist. I began compiling my favorite recipes, ingredients, and decor sources, and created planning tools and cheat sheets to help others draw out their creative spirits. My hope is that this book will serve as your go-to party-planning resource, a place for finding ideas, making notes, and creating memories to last a lifetime.

My other hope for this book is that it will inspire others to celebrate more often and see magic in everyday moments. Our fast-paced culture has fewer and fewer rituals. Inviting friends and family over for dinner to mark the passing of another year or a great accomplishment are our new rituals, and this book will help you find deeper, more creative ways to honor and celebrate a beloved friend, family member, or coworker—or the best person of all: yourself.

In *Trophy Cupcakes and Parties!*, I've included my best cupcake-baking tricks and techniques, a "Party Planning 101" chapter (including must-have cheat sheets for making the planning process easy and inspired), crafting and party "Pro-Tips" sprinkled throughout, my treasured source list of the absolute best ingredients and resources (see page 221), and five festive chapters of my favorite party themes explaining how to re-create them and make them your own.

I truly believe everyone has the ingenuity to create his or her own beautiful celebrations. Sometimes it just takes a bit of prodding toward that possibly cobwebbed door marked "Your Imagination." My favorite key to that door is baking decadent, delicious cupcakes. Try it yourself, and hearken that magical world of fanciful parties where anything's possible.

Jennifer Shea

Founder, baker, party-maker, Trophy Cupcakes and Party

PARTY PLANNING 101

How to make it a magical party.

Planning a party is all about honoring someone you love, with a healthy dose of yummy food and fun decor included in the tribute. But a truly wow-worthy party—the kind that people will be talking about for years to come—is not that much more effort than one featuring a couple of balloons and a handful of streamers. Honest! Whether you're looking to blow your guests away or simply add a little dazzle to an annual event, the steps to consider are always the same.

The secret weapon behind every epic bash is a terrific theme. The trick lies in finding ways to capitalize on that theme and take it to new, resplendent heights. So let's get started! In this section we'll go through the planning process step-by-step, including a worksheet and fun questionnaire that will get your imagination going, tips on selecting the theme, must-have party elements, cupcake ideas (of course!), and no-fail hosting rules. By the end of this chapter, you'll have the basic know-how for forging ahead into party-planning land.

The first matter, though, is choosing a theme. Not just any theme, but a Truly Terrific Theme. Well, how do you do that? Truly Terrific Themes can be very straightforward, such as a favorite color, or they can be complex, such as interpreting an abstract concept. "Graduation." "Birthday." "Anniversary." Those aren't themes; they're events. The idea behind a theme is to think *beyond* the event you're celebrating. Think of your theme as the event's headline, something that forms a clear vision to guide you through the planning process. To help you pinpoint a Truly Terrific Theme, I created a short questionnaire you can give to the guest—or guests—of honor to illuminate their likes (and dislikes) and basically figure out what makes them tick. (Planning a surprise party? You may need to perform covert operations and oh-so-casually drop these questions into conversation, or ask friends and family.) For young guests it might be easier to interview your guest of honor to gather answers for the Truly Terrific Theme Generator. For really little kids, like one- and two-year olds, ask parents to fill out the questionnaire with all of the young one's favorite things.

The first four questions are general: who, what, where, and when? And they may be more appropriate for you to fill out rather than the guest of honor, but don't underestimate the basics, as you might very well find your theme right there! A great location (see Location, Location, Location, page 12) or especially festive day of the year, for instance, can form the foundation for a Truly Terrific Theme.

The next questions get into the nitty-gritty, to tap into the guest of honor's more thoughtful side. You might want to simplify, vary, or omit some of them, depending on the party girl or boy (you obviously won't interview your one-year-old about her favorite era), but this form should cover the bases for most people. The following chapters will illustrate in more depth how to bring your theme to life, but first things first: copy or scan and print the opposite page (or visit the Printables section of TrophyCupcakes.com/book), and work on getting answers to the questions.

Once the Truly Terrific Theme Generator is filled out, you'll have a lot of great inspiration to work with—from the guest of honor's favorite color (see Color: Aqua Pool Party, page 51) to favorite character (see Superhero Training Camp Party, page 101). Pick something fun and unique from the list, an element that will put a big smile on the guest of honor's face. You might even find it hard at this point to choose just *one* idea from all the information you've gathered. If you're struggling, ask friends or family or even the honoree—most people are thrilled to be in on it!

Turn the page to see a sample of a filled-out Truly Terrific Theme Generator. If I were throwing a party for this guest of honor, I'd have lots of inspiration. I could create a party out of every single answer—or by combining a few. The theme could be built around Northwest Living (passion) with plenty of local oysters to go around. Or, why not a fab Palm Springs (favorite place) party, complete with paper lanterns hanging in every corner. To get an idea of how to make themes such as these come to life, explore the Away We Go! (page 69) or Pastimes & Passions (page 149) chapters.

TRULY TERRIFIC THEME GENERATOR

The Basics

Who (guest of honor): ....

What (the event): ....

Where: ....

When: ....

My Favorite Things

Food(s): ....

Drink(s): ....

Cake/Dessert: ....

Color: ....

Book: ....

Movie/TV show: ....

Band/Musician/Style of music: ....

Era (roaring '20s, disco '70s, new wave '80s, etc.): ....

....

Place to travel or dream destination: ....

Hobbies or passions (gardening, skateboarding, persimmons, ballet, cooking, travel, etc.):

....

Character (from a movie or book), imaginary friend (unicorn, superhero, Hello Kitty, etc.), or historical figure (artist, writer, inventor, etc.):

....

Dislikes

Any food allergies or unique party phobias? ....

....

TRULY TERRIFIC THEME GENERATOR

The Basics

Who (guest of honor): JORI DAVIS

What (the event): 40th BIRTHDAY

Where: PALM ROOM

When: MARCH 20th

My Favorite Things

Food(s): OYSTERS

Drink(s): CHAMPAGNE

Cake/Dessert: HUMMINGBIRD

Color: GREEN!

Book: TIM WALKER PICTURES

Movie/TV show: AMELIE'

Band/Musician/Style of music: BEYONCE, JT, DANCE

Era (roaring '20s, disco '70s, new wave '80s, etc.): 80's

Place to travel or dream destination: PALM SPRINGS

Hobbies or passions (gardening, skateboarding, persimmons, ballet, cooking, travel, etc.):

NW LIVING, PAPER LANTERNS

Character (from a movie or book), imaginary friend (unicorn, superhero, Hello Kitty, etc.), or historical figure (artist, writer, inventor, etc.):

SOFIA COPPOLA'S MARIE ANTOINETTE

Dislikes

Any food allergies or unique party phobias? PHOBIA: SURPRISE PARTIES!!

The Five Must-Do's for Great Parties

Once you've chosen a theme, it's time to plan the specifics of your party. You'll find clear and easy directions throughout the book. But if you're feeling overwhelmed, delegate! (See Ask for Help, page 17.) Ask a friend, hire a neighbor, or purchase what you need from a local bakery, party shop, or online. You could even delegate all five must-do's and still pull off a great party. Now that's savvy party planning!

SET THE STAGE

- I like to start the planning with decor (including a color palette), because it creates the entire look and atmosphere of the party. Coco Chanel once said, "Fashion is not something that exists in dresses only. Fashion is in the sky, in the street, fashion has to do with ideas, the way we live, what is happening." With all due respect to Chanel, I think of decor in the same way she thinks of fashion. Decor isn't just the balloons you hang from the ceiling—it's in the invitation, the props, the favors, and even the location. Decor can be simple and focused on one corner of the room, or extravagant, with the entire space transformed from top to bottom. I'll leave it up to you how far you want to take it; the important thing is, as with fashion, to set a mood.

Go for Color

- Choose a color palette and use it shamelessly. Think invitations, napkins, balloons, plates, streamers, confetti, and favors. Add a pop of color—a bright, vivid tone that contrasts with neutrals—into your palette wherever you can.

- If you struggle with choosing a gorgeous and creative color palette, books are a great resource for finding images and inspiration. When I planned my son Fleetwood's Circus Party, I looked at five or six vintage books about circuses and found my colors there. Natural objects are also a great color source. Look at the sea, citrus fruits, a landscape, or a flower arrangement and jot down pleasing color combinations. For the Destination: Hawaii party (page 88), the colors came straight from nature, specifically tropical flowers and leaves, koa wood, and shells. Another favorite color source is fashion. Copy colors from a favorite party dress or textile print, or straight off the pages of a fashion magazine (you can find amazing color combinations in vintage fashion magazines at your local library). Need more color inspiration? Check out "The Perfect Palette" on Pinterest.

PRO-TIP

If you rent a venue, be sure to ask in advance what kinds of decorations are allowed. You don't want to plan on lighting candles or taping decor to the walls, only to find out such things are a no-go on the day of the party.

Decorate

- The rest of this book will give you lots of ideas, and I'm betting you'll begin to see inspiration all around you once you have decor on your mind. In a nutshell, you want to first choose a color palette that fits your theme, and then start brainstorming design elements—such as props, papers, flowers and fabrics, lighting and accessories—that underscore your theme. Run with it and definitely have fun!

- **Customize, and When the Mood Strikes, Be Obsessive.** Adding a special design element—anything from a simple polka dot to a monogram or a number—that guests will see throughout the party, from the invitation right down to the favors, takes decor from just plain pretty to oh-my-gosh impressive. Think about a sweet butterfly shape for a garden party, a metallic "50" for a golden anniversary, a graphic pine cone for a camping party, a beautiful monogram of your mom's first initial for her birthday or Mother's Day, or a retro beach ball for a summer pool party.

- **Location, Location, Location.** Decor can be inspired (or dictated) by your party's venue. Keeping your guest count in mind, get creative with your party location! A camping-themed party begs for a big backyard, park, or campsite (see Camping Party, page 167). A grand engagement party feels perfect in a sophisticated space such as a large home or ballroom. And a pool, skating, or ballet party will be way more fun in a local venue dedicated to the pastime.

- **Invitations Set the Tone.** You know your color palette, your location, and your theme, so the next order of business is creating an invitation. An invite, of course, announces the who, what, why, when, and where. But even more importantly, it sets the tone for the party, gives guests a sneak peek into the revelry, provides clues on what to wear (see Dress Your Guests, page 43), and sets expectations. Be sure to find or create an invitation that represents the theme of the party, such as the gold confetti invite for our Sparkle: Engagement Party (page 43), or a handmade paper lei invitation for the Destination: Hawaii party (page 88).

  I have a long-standing obsession with paper—old-fashioned paper invitations, to be exact—because there's something special about a real-life envelope arriving at your home that e-mail cannot replace. Local paper shops offer write-in invites as well as custom options, and I love Minted.com's adorable customizable paper invites. That being said, I do use e-mail invitations for parties—PaperlessPost.com is a favorite—because I love how such sites track RSVPs, attach maps, and send reminders. If you have time to send paper invites and the wherewithal to track RSVPs, I recommend it. If not, e-invites can be a great way to go.

PRO-TIP

You'll want to give your guests enough time to save the date, so send invitations two to four weeks prior to the occasion. If out-of-town guests are invited, six to eight weeks is preferable.

GET CRAFTY

OK, I can hear you saying, "It's hard enough planning a party, now you want me to get crafty too?" I admit that adding handcrafted elements might seem daunting to some, but, when time allows, I always encourage that special, do-it-yourself touch, whether it's a decor element, favors, or a game or activity. The elements made with love—and by hand—are the ones people will be talking about forever after and will cement your reputation as World's Best Party Thrower. In each of the upcoming chapters, I offer ideas and instructions for classic and simple, but impressive, crafts that will take your party from ordinary to outstanding!

ENTERTAIN THEM

The guests have arrived—now what? You need to decide what will *happen* at the party. If your party is about being social—mingling, eating, and drinking—then music is the only addition I'd recommend. Music not only sets the mood, it can also make or break an event. Therefore, choose wisely. (See How to Make a Playlist, page 14.) For a really special celebration, a DJ or live band is always a hit.

Also consider activities. If the event is for kids, what are they going to do for three hours? On a sunny day, a big backyard might be all you need. When that's not the case, you'll want to come up with a themed game, craft, or activity for the group. Hire a magician or face painter, plan outdoor games like three-legged races and a beanbag toss, or throw the party at a pool, skating rink, or somewhere with a built-in activity.

Favors and gift bags are small tokens given to guests to show appreciation for their attendance. They're a thoughtful way to say thank you and leave guests with one final, special touch to remember the event by. For a kid's party, you might want to have a goody bag filled with cute trinkets (parents usually appreciate toys or healthy snacks over candy-filled bags, though I'm not a big fan of cheap plastic toys that end up in landfills). For grown-ups, a take-away could be a small plant, a jar of homemade jam or other treat, or a small container of candies for the ride home.

Now that all your elements are in place, use the Trophy-Worthy Party Planner (page 16) to keep track of details. Copy or scan and print the planner (or visit the Printables section of TrophyCupcakes.com/book) so you'll have it with you when you shop for supplies.

PRO-TIP

To encourage party flow, place the food, drinks/bar, and dessert table in three separate areas.

SERVE UP BITES & SIPS

Naturally, the guest of honor's answer to "favorite food and drink" should provide some great ideas for menu planning. But not every party is thrown to honor one special person (and their favorite food might not be a crowd-pleaser), so consider what foods will enhance your theme and be a hit with guests. Take into account the guests' ages and the time of day. Sometimes certain snacks and foods are simply a must dictated by the theme. For example, my Camping Party (page 167) features s'mores and grilled hot dogs, while the Destination: Paris party (page 71) naturally lends itself to French cheeses and champagne.

- Basically, the thoughtful host or hostess doesn't let guests go hungry. A few food stations strategically scattered around the party space, or a nice big buffet, will allow people to nibble as they please. I offer food and drink suggestions for all the parties in the book.

How to Make a Playlist

- Think about making a party soundtrack. Music is essential to getting guests in the spirit and creating the mood you envision. To get on the right track, ask yourself a few questions:

What kind of mood do I want to create?

- Mood is key. Whether you want an upbeat dance party, a mellow get-together, or a sophisticated gathering, you'll need to start by finding a few songs or artists that represent the mood.
- Once you have a few songs in mind, find more music with the same vibe either in your own music library or online. There are lots of fantastic services to help you find music similar to the songs or artists you've zeroed in on. Try out iLike.com, the iTunes genius feature, Pandora.com, TheFilter.com, or TasteKid.com.

What's the theme of my event and how can music add to that theme?

- If you're throwing a thematic party, think about how you can use music to enhance the experience. For example, for our Destination: Mexico party, we created a playlist that consists of hip Latin American tunes and Latin-influenced indie rock (see page 83). Other themes work similarly. For a superhero party, download a bunch of movie soundtracks from classics like *Superman*. This will add to the drama and to the theme! For something like a baby shower, think about the guest of honor's preferred style of music, and play it softly in the background.

Do I want people tapping their feet and dancing, or do I want something subtle that fades into the background so guests can talk the night away?

- The volume and popularity of your tunes will be key here—whether you are creating a dance-party or just adding some ambience. For a festive affair like a birthday or cocktail party, you'll want to turn the volume up fairly high so guests feel the fun the moment they walk in the door. Hold off on playing sing-along type of tunes (such as popular Top 40 hits) until you really want people up and dancing.
- Now that you've got a playlist plan, load twenty or more songs (based on how long your party will last) onto an iPod (or your device of choice), and hit "play."

GIVE THEM CUPCAKES

- For me, cake in some form is a nonnegotiable element of every party. I simply love cake and its history. Did you know that cake has been around for almost as long as flour itself? And that sweet, flour-based, baked desserts have been associated with celebrations for almost as long? The ancient Greeks offered cake to their gods, and medieval bakers made festive fruitcakes that lasted for months. Most sources say cupcakes were invented in the United States, in the early nineteenth century, as a way to bake individual cakes in small pottery cups. Um, genius! Although I still sometimes serve traditional cakes and other desserts at my parties, cupcakes are, obviously, my favorite. They're so easy to serve, and they make party-perfect canvases for any theme's flavors and decor.
- A Hawaiian-themed party (page 88), for example, looks (and tastes!) better with Piña Colada Cupcakes (page 94), hand-piped with swirls of Coconut Rum Buttercream topped with a maraschino cherry and a little paper umbrella. A *Casablanca* Party (page 133) deserves *Casablanca* Cupcakes (page 137)—Moroccan-inspired orange-and-almond cupcakes topped with rose-kissed buttercream. I provide scrumptious recipes for themed cupcakes in every chapter.

Five No-Fail Tips for How to Be the Quintessential Trophy Hostess

Before you send the first invitation, let's review a basic tenet of parties: hosting. I like to call the perfect party planner a Trophy Hostess, but feel free to switch that up, depending on your gender!

Know Thyself. Stay within your comfort zone. Don't get elaborate if planning is overwhelming your time or creeping beyond your budget. Some of the best parties I've attended have been simple and low-key with just one or two well-thought-out details. Be realistic about your time and resources, and your party will be a hit. Bigger is not always better.

Know Thy Guests. A wonderful hostess makes guests feel welcome and comfortable from the moment the invitation arrives, all through the event, up to the moment they walk out the door. The invitation is courteous, letting guests know what to expect: what to wear, whether to bring gifts or not, where and when the party starts and ends, and what will be served.

A TROPHY HOSTESS IS:

- Well prepared
- Generous (glasses are kept full and enough food is available for all)
- Always making sure guests feel welcome and comfortable
- All about having a fabulous time at her or his own parties

TROPHY-WORTHY PARTY PLANNER

Use this planner (and the Truly Terrific Theme Generator, page 9) to keep all of your party details in one handy-dandy place. Not only will it help you feel confident you've covered all your bases, but it can also be a big help when you shop for supplies.

The Details

Theme: ....

Decor: ....

Color palette: ....

Design element(s): ....

Invitations: ....

Bites and sips for adults: ....

Bites and sips for kids: ....

Cupcake flavor and decorations: ....

Entertainment (music, games, activities): ....

....

Favors/gift bags: ....

Key contacts—phone numbers and e-mail addresses: ....

....

....

....

Supplies needed: ....

....

....

Notes: ....

....

....

....

A Trophy Hostess plans every detail based on the guest of honor and the guests. Toddler parties should be planned around naptime. Tweens will probably want to choose their own music. Friends and the guest of honor might want to participate in the planning in some way, and a Trophy Hostess doesn't get territorial. But overall, manage your expectations for guests in terms of preparation and participation. You don't want the party to be a cause of stress for others.

Ask for Help—or Delegate, Delegate, Delegate. There are plenty of reasons to enlist the help of others. Maybe "spare time" isn't in your vocabulary. Perhaps you love crafting but don't fancy yourself a baker. Don't worry. Focus on what you're good at (and what you have time for), then delegate the rest for party success.

For larger affairs, enlisting a caterer or professional entertainment may be in order.

Many artists, crafters, party planners, and detail-oriented folks tend to be control freaks (I'm 100 percent guilty). We have huge ideas and think it will be easier to do everything ourselves. If you're one of these people, know this: the chance of having a successful party—and one that you'll actually enjoy—is exponentially higher when you have help on board.

Be Prepared. Coordinating the details ahead of time and finishing advance preparation will make for a stress-free day. For example, I prepare favors or goody bags as far in advance as possible. I also choose menu items that are easy or can be prepped or made a day or two ahead—or even frozen weeks in advance. Set up everything you can the night before, if the space allows it. Also, get an early start and get ready well in advance. Setting up always takes twice as long as you think it will. I can't tell you how many times I've frantically put on my makeup and cocktail dress five minutes before guests are arriving. Ideally, everything should be done an hour before the party starts so you have not one ounce of frazzle in you when guests arrive.

Have Fun—or What's the Point? The most important thing to do is have fun and feel fabulous. If *you're* having a great time, your guests will too. This means you must follow steps 1 through 4, no excuses! Remember: The Trophy Hostess entertains to have fun, meet new people, show others a good time—and, of course, celebrate and honor a wonderful, worthy, special guest of honor.

Stock your Party Pantry!

Every party planner should have a "pantry" of basic (but essential and wonderful!) items on hand . . . so you're ready to craft up a party storm at a moment's notice or on a whim. With these party and craft must-haves, you'll be partying in no time!

My Top 10 Party Pantry Essentials

Crepe Paper. Italian crepe paper rolls (Cartefini is my favorite brand) and old-fashioned crepe paper streamers and folds in a rainbow of colors.

Tissue Paper Decorations. Also in a rainbow of colors. Types like honeycomb balls and paper fans can be hung quickly, and happen to be my favorite.

Confetti. The key to turning a ho-hum table into an instant party. I make mine in custom colors from pretty tissue and one-inch craft punch. Just sandwich a stack of about ten pieces of tissue between plain copy paper, then punch. I also love edible candy confetti sprinkles!

Candles. Birthday candles, of course. (I literally carry them in my handbag.) But keep votives and tapers on hand, too, for instant ambiance.

Tableware. A dozen each of champagne and wine glasses, a stack of white appetizer/cake plates, several large platters or trays, and linen napkins as well as pretty paper party plates and napkins in a variety of designs.

Ribbon. A variety of gorgeous ribbons in various widths—Midori Ribbon is my absolute fave! Use it to finish off gorgeous gifts, make napkins rings, tie bows, or to hang decorations.

Straws and Swizzle Sticks. Especially stripy paper straws, which are great for both sipping and crafting.

Vases. A collection of decorative vases in various sizes. I love small ones that only hold a couple of stems—making life easy for *pluck*-and-play floral design.

Chilling Bin and Ice Bucket. A stylish chilling bin is a nice thing to have on hand to class-up an instant bar. Add an ice bucket and tongs, and you're a total pro.

Chilled Champagne. Keep a bottle of bubbly in your refrigerator at all times for life's unexpected celebrations.

PRO-TIP

Organize these items by type, and store them in clear, labeled bins so you can always find them quickly.

My Top 10 Craft Essentials

Paper. Good old construction, tissue, and crepe paper are a must, but I really love handmade sheets of paper in a variety of gorgeous patterns for wrapping gifts, making decorations, and, of course, crafting cupcake picks (see Pro Tip, page 61).

Tape. Double-sided is a must (I need stock in the stuff), as well as scotch, masking, and lots of decorative washi tape! Floral tape is also essential for making quick nosegays, boutonnieres, and corsages.

Scissors, Snips, and Cutters. A small, sharp, fine-tipped pair, an industrial "will cut anything" pair, a pair of floral sheers, small wire cutters, an X-acto knife, a pair of pinking shears, a rotary cutter, and my favorite: fringe scissors!

Glue. Hot glue (of course!), glue sticks, Tacky Glue, Mod Podge, and classic Elmer's glue.

Needle and Thread. (And, ideally, a sewing machine.) It's helpful to have a variety of needles, including a large quilting needle or lei needle for stringing flowers, cupcake liners (page 155), or other decorations.

Craft Punches. As many styles and sizes as you've got room for. Include a small hole-punch in your stash, for hanging decorations.

Twine and Trims. I love striped baker's twine and good ol' natural twine from the hardware store. Don't forget rickrack and pom-pom trim, perfect for embellishing birthday hats.

Wire. Thin-gauge wire for floral arrangements, and securing things in general.

Self-Healing Mat. Essential surface for cutting templates or using a rotary cutter to make large fringe garland (page 116) and all types of crafts.

Glitter. I like the vintage-looking kind with a coarser chop (German glass glitter), which is not suitable for kids crafts, however, any glitter will do!

Toasting Tips

Toasting is a wonderful way to acknowledge the guest of honor and the special event being celebrated—and it can be as easy as singing "Happy Birthday." Whether it's a birthday, summer party, or an anniversary, gather around the guest of honor or host to raise a glass, sing a song, or say thank you. It's a time-honored tradition that we could all use more of.

A toast doesn't *need* to include the raising of glasses. It can simply be getting everyone's attention, thanking them for their friendship, and letting them know you're happy they could be there. As I've said before, so many of us don't fully embrace the special moments in our busy lives. Why not start by throwing more parties? And instead of letting guests leave without a toast, gather everyone up and let them know they're all special to you—special enough that you threw a party!

Here are some general guidelines to make your toasts both sweet and successful:

- The first toast should be made by the host.
- Be sure to stand and name the guest of honor (and/or the event). Feel free to stay seated for intimate casual gatherings.
- Funny and witty stories are fun for everyone, but only if they're in good taste.
- Plan ahead for formal toasts. Consult toasting websites and books for samples of great toasts but be sincere and express your true feelings.
- Don't forget to end your toast with a hearty callout, such as: "Cheers!," "All the best!," "Happy Birthday!," or "Here's to you!"

A WORD TO TOASTEES

If you're being toasted, be gracious and accept the accolades or showering of affection with style and grace. It's customary to stay seated until the end of the toast and to not drink to yourself. Simply stand and say thank you, and propose your own toast if you like. One good turn deserves another!

Ultra Power
Solid State Speed Control

TROPHY'S TECHNIQUES, TIPS & TRICKS

Tried-and-true cupcake baking and decorating tips.

I believe in taking the time to make things by hand, crafting both for personal pleasure and for the ones you love. To carry on the tradition of simply making something—anything—is a truly worthy goal.

As you read this book, you'll see that I'm obsessed with all kinds of crafts, though baking is my first love. To me, crafting butter and flour into an edible masterpiece that triggers sheer delight is pretty magical stuff!

Most people think baking is hard, but the good news is, it's *not*. True, it takes practice and time to master, but the wonderful secret is that anyone can do it, so long as they're armed with a few tips and are schooled on potential pitfalls. That's why I'm going to share my best baking and decorating tips, and advise you on how to stock your pantry with everything you need to make cupcakes like a pro. The time and effort will be worth it when you see everyone's eyes light up after you serve them the best kind of cupcakes on the planet: homemade.

1. Mixing Bowls
2. Cupcake Pans
3. Stand Mixer
4. Rubber Spatulas
5. Portion Scoop
6. Pretty Baking Cups
7. Toppings + Tints
8. Offset Spatula
9. Pastry Bag + Tips
10. Mesh Sieve

Top 5 Essential Cupcake Tools

You probably have the basic equipment you need to make wonderful cupcakes at home. At the very least, you can conjure delicious cupcakes using a cupcake pan, a few big bowls, a rubber spatula, cupcake liners, and measuring cups and spoons. However, if you want to make your cupcakes truly Trophy-worthy, here are the essential tools I recommend.

Stand Mixer. Now, my grandmother would say that mixing by hand—no mixer, just a wooden spoon and a lot of elbow grease!—is the only way to go. However, if you bake a lot or want to bake in larger quantities (and reduce cramping in your arm, Grandma!), a stand mixer is simply a dreamy tool. Mine is a KitchenAid, and it quite literally changed my life (see below). A stand mixer will save you time and free up your hands for things like cracking eggs while the butter is creaming or lining pans while ingredients are incorporating. It will also help you keep your counters tidy.

High-Quality Cupcake Pans. (Also called *muffin pans*, *muffin tins*, or *cupcake tins*.) Best-quality pans are just as important as best-quality ingredients, and heavyweight, shiny pans, like Chicago Metallic and Cuisinart, work best for cupcakes. Dark and nonstick pans absorb extra heat and can quickly overbake cupcakes; if you're using these types of pans, always reduce the oven temperature by 25 degrees and check on the cupcakes a few minutes earlier than the recipes call for.

I recommend having at least two 12-cup pans (the wells should hold ½ cup batter) so that you don't have to wait for your pan to cool before baking the rest of the batter. I keep four 12-cup pans at home so I can make quick work of a double batch. I also have two mini cupcake pans with two dozen wells per pan for the days when tinier treats are in order. Large or "Texas-size" extra-large cupcake pans exist, but I prefer standard, 3-inch cupcakes. If I'm craving something larger, I tend to just make a cake.

HOW A MIXER CHANGED MY LIFE

Annajean "Skitty" Goldsmith was a wonderful woman and good friend who encouraged me to follow my dreams, and gave me a chrome KitchenAid mixer for Christmas more than ten years ago. Although I had a decent kitchen setup by that time, her gift was like receiving a brand new car. (Let's just say that my baking tools were of the Honda variety, and this KitchenAid felt like a Ferrari.) I can still remember barely being able to believe I had such a beautiful piece of machinery in my kitchen. All my hopes and dreams of someday owning my own bakery were in that KitchenAid box. Skitty's generous and thoughtful gift sent me on my way to perfecting Trophy's cupcake recipes and eventually creating my own shop. Shortly after I opened Trophy Cupcakes and Party, that same mixer accompanied me (in my suitcase) to New York City to bake cupcakes for Martha Stewart in my friend's tiny Manhattan kitchen. My KitchenAid is pretty beat up now and missing the speed-control knob, but it still mixes like a dream and I wouldn't think of replacing it.

Yes, it's possible to love a mixer. Thank you, Skitty. That single gift changed my life.

Mesh Sieve. (Also called a *flour sieve, sifter*, or *wire strainer*.) Sifted confectioners' sugar is essential for creamy, lump-free buttercream. I use a 10-inch Camford stainless steel mesh sieve (available at Sur la Table) with a long handle on one side and a hanging hook on the other, so I can rest it across the bowl as I sift. Mine doubles as a strainer, which is good for everything from making sure custard is lump-free (see Lavender Crème Brûlée Cupcakes, page 78) to rinsing quinoa and draining pasta, and it's much easier to use than a hand-crank or squeeze sifter.

Heavy Mixing Bowls. Serious bakers need a great set of mixing bowls in various sizes. I have a variety of stainless steel mixing bowls I've collected over the years. The sizes range from extra large (12 quarts), which are great for collecting sifted ingredients, to very small (½ quart), great for cracking eggs. If you're buying a set of bowls for the first time, choose heavy-duty stainless steel nesting bowls: a good set will last you a lifetime. The one with lids are very nice; I especially love All-Clad's set of 3-, 5-, and 7-quart bowls. There are also plenty of good bowl sets out there that are more economical. Just look for bowls that are labeled "professional quality" or feel heavy when you pick them up, and you're good to go.

PRO-TIP

More tools to help you make Trophy-worthy cupcakes: a kitchen torch, an apple corer, a whisk, a citrus zester, and a reamer.

Heavy-Duty Rubber Spatula. Scraping down batter and buttercream sounds like a job for a cheap rubber tool, but a really good rubber spatula will make easy work of this repetitive task that is such a big part of cupcake making. I like the heatproof silicone variety because they're very versatile; you can use them for stirring custards or melting chocolate, or for whipping up scrambled eggs or a stir-fry.

Trophy's Five Fave Tips for Amazing Cupcakes

The number-one question I'm asked on a daily basis is, "How do you make Trophy cupcakes taste so good?" There's no one simple answer but a handful of secrets. Well, they're not actually *secrets*, just tips that professional bakers learn over time, and I'd love to share my favorites with you.

Use Trophy-Worthy Ingredients. Always start with the very best ingredients. Nothing will create so-so cupcakes like so-so ingredients. So if you want your cupcakes to taste like Trophy's, take the time to find the very best. (If nothing else, use the best cocoa powder, butter, vanilla, and dairy products you can find.)

At Trophy, we use **Valrhona cocoa powder** from France (widely recognized as the best cocoa in the world) and **Nielsen-Massey Madagascar Bourbon pure vanilla extract** (again, the best!). (Fun fact! There is no bourbon in Madagascar Bourbon vanilla. The name refers to the Bourbon Islands where it is grown.) Butter that's made from milk given by happy cows absolutely tastes better, so we only use **local, hormone-free dairy products**

1
2
3
4
5
6
7
8
9
10
11
1. Local Washington apples 2. Fleur de sel 3. Local, hormone-free milk 4. Local, hormone-free butter 5. Cacao Barry French chocolate flakes 6. Callebaut Belgian bittersweet chocolate 7. Organic farmers' market blueberries 8. Fresh lemons 9. Local, cage-free eggs 10. Nielsen-Massey Madagascar Bourbon vanilla 11. Valrhona cocoa

from Washington cows. **Cacao Barry French chocolate flakes** are beyond compare. Belgian **Callebaut chocolate** is my favorite for making buttercream, but there are many wonderful chocolates; look for high-quality dark chocolate with 50 to 70 percent cacao (cocoa bean solids). We use Callebaut 60 percent. Experiment with different chocolates until you find your personal favorite. **Organic produce** is excellent, especially for zesting lemons and limes. And bake with whatever's **in season**—we use yams and apples in the autumn, for example, and organic berries from our local farmers' markets all summer long.

Start with Room Temperature Ingredients. Unless the recipe calls for cold ingredients, bring your ingredients to room temperature. Doing so helps ingredients blend faster and more evenly into the batter (and buttercream). Uneven mixing contributes to overmixing, which creates tough, dry cupcakes (see Mix Properly, below). So take butter, eggs, milk, and other cold ingredients out of the refrigerator 30 minutes prior to using them. If you're in a hurry or forget to do this, you can place eggs in a bowl of warm (not hot) water for 10 minutes and gently heat milk or cream just until the chill is off (do not let it get warm). You can also bring butter to room temperature by microwaving it in 10-second increments until it's *just* room temperature: be careful not to melt it.

PRO-TIP

Never crack eggs directly into the batter. Always crack eggs into a clean bowl first, then add them to the batter to avoid eggshells (or a bad egg!) in your cupcakes.

Mix Properly. Mixing ingredients for too long is the main reason cupcakes can turn out tough or dry (boo!). Overbaking and bad recipes are culprits too.

You don't have to worry too much about overmixing when you're creaming butter and adding eggs; the problems occur once you add dry ingredients to the batter, because the longer flour is mixed, the more gluten is produced. Some gluten is good; it gives cupcakes structure. Too much gluten, though, makes cakes tough instead of tender. So, when the recipe says, "Do not overmix," mix the dry ingredients until the batter has *just* come together—you might even see a bit of unmixed flour, but no big streaks. I wish I could give you an exact time to mix, but everyone's mixer is different (stand mixers mix faster than hand ones, and all is dependent on speed). You simply have to practice and develop an eye for it.

Measure Accurately. When you're cooking a meal, you can throw in a few extra ingredients—a pinch of this, a handful of that—and still have amazing results. Baking, however, is a *science*, and precise measuring is essential to achieving Trophy results.

For starters, use good-quality measuring cups and spoons. I choose heavy-duty stainless steel for my measuring cups and spoons because they won't get warped or dented like lighter metals or plastic. Glass measuring cups, like the ones from Pyrex, are perfect for measuring liquids because again, they won't warp, and you can see the liquid you are measuring through the glass. A 2-cup is a great size! Don't use heaping cups or spoons for any of your dry ingredients—level them carefully with the back of a flat butter knife. Measure liquid ingredients in liquid measuring cups placed on a flat, even surface to be sure you get an accurate line.

With those measuring basic tips in mind and a little experience under your belt, I encourage creativity! Once you've mastered a basic recipe, or if you're already an experienced baker, have fun and throw in a pinch of this or that to make your cupcakes truly your own.

Don't Overbake. In other words, watch your cupcakes like a hawk! Overbaking and overmixing are equal-opportunity offenders in the world of dry cupcakes (a place I like to call "Cupcake Hell"). At home, I only put one 12-cup pan in the oven at a time, so I can be sure my cupcakes are baking evenly. Depending on the recipe, they generally take between 15 and 25 minutes to bake. If your recipe says 20 minutes, take a quick peek at 12 minutes, just in case. (If your oven door is glass, turn the light on and look without opening the oven so you don't disrupt the heat.) If you see that half of the cupcakes are rising or firming up much faster than the other half, open the oven and rotate the pan. Check again at 15 minutes. You'll know they need more time if the batter looks wet or wobbly. Check again at 17 minutes.

If the cupcakes have risen and look like they're possibly done, take a closer look right away. Use a wooden skewer or a toothpick to test for doneness by poking one of the center cupcakes all the way to the bottom. If it comes out with wet batter, the cupcakes need more time. If there are a few crumbs but no wet batter—*yay*! The cupcakes are done, so take them out immediately. If the skewer comes out completely clean (unless the recipe says otherwise!), you may have overbaked them. The cupcakes will still continue to bake after you take them out of the oven, so in most cases it's important to remove them before the skewer comes out completely clean.

Also, be sure your oven temperature is correct. A too-hot oven can overbake your cupcakes, cause them to rise like a volcano (instead of a nice dome), or even make them rise, then fall. If you are having any of these problems, lower your oven's temperature by 25 degrees the next time. I also highly recommend using an oven thermometer to be certain of your particular oven's true temperature.

FRESH IS BEST!

Whenever possible, bake your cupcakes on the same day you'll be serving them. Freshly baked cupcakes always taste best (unless the recipe says otherwise). If you need to bake them the day before, wrap the unfrosted cupcakes tightly in plastic wrap and store them at room temperature. Buttercream can be made fresh or made in advance and stored in the refrigerator for up to a week. Simply bring it to room temperature, then rewhip it before frosting your cupcakes.

Five Must-Haves for Your Decorating Pantry

Offset Spatula. Offset spatulas—small angled metal spatulas with a flexible blade—make frosting a breeze. Mine is an Ateco with a wooden handle and 4½-inch blade, and it's probably my favorite go-to cupcake-decorating tool. It can be used to create a variety of looks, from buttercream "waves" to a perfectly smooth surface (essential for writing "Happy Birthday!"; see Trophy Frosting Techniques, page 32). Offset spatulas are also the perfect decorating tool for small children who can't quite get their hands around a pastry bag yet.

Pastry Bags and Tips. Yes, it's possible to make a pastry bag out of a resealable plastic bag. But if you're serious about hand-piping cupcakes, I would recommend investing in a few good reusable pastry bags. I love Ateco's "Wunderbag." It has a cotton exterior, which provides a good grip, even with buttery hands, and a coated interior that washes clean so you can use it over and over again. I like 18-inch bags best—any bigger than that, and it can be difficult to squeeze the buttercream through and still have control over the piping. Smaller 10- or 12-inch bags filled half full are best for children's hands.

An array of sturdy metal pastry tips for piping fancy shapes and designs is a must for professional-style cupcake decorating. Even the simplest round- or star-shaped tip can take your cupcakes from everyday to showstopping. If you're just starting out, invest in a small kit, such as one from Ateco, with five basic tips: extra-large round, extra-large star, small round (for writing), small star, and medium flower. Or treat yourself to a deluxe kit with more variety if you really want to go pro.

NOTE: Tip-size numbers can vary from brand to brand. At Trophy we use Ateco tips, so all tip-size references in this book are based on Ateco's numbering system.

Portion Scoops. A portion scoop looks like an ice cream scoop and has a spring-loaded blade that scrapes out its contents. I use a 1- to 1½-ounce scoop to portion out buttercream equally on hand-frosted and "rolled" (see Trophy Frosting Techniques, page 32) cupcakes. Using a scoop makes the finished cupcakes look more consistent (thus more professional). And they're handy to keep in the kitchen for portioning batter for uniform cupcakes and cookies too.

Pretty Baking Cups. (Also called *cupcake liners*, *muffin liners*, or *fairy cups*.) Baking cups are one of the main reasons making cupcakes is easy and fun. The "wrapper" portions each cake, makes cleanup easy, and eliminates greased pans, plates, and forks. Each cupcake is a perfect little package in your hand!

Thanks to cupcakes' popularity, the days of choosing among just foil, white, or pastel baking cups are long gone. Although I love the simple, fluted grocery store–style cups and use them often, you can find patterns to complement just about any color palette or party theme with resources such as BakeItPretty.com. The options are endless and adorable, so have fun experimenting!

Toppings and Tints. First, let's talk about toppings. Make your cupcakes the centerpiece of the party with toppings such as sanding sugar, dragées, nonpareils, miniature candies and chocolate chips, edible flowers and herbs, candied fruits and zests, cupcake picks

Toppings Glossary

When it comes to toppings, the world of cupcakes sometimes has its own language. Here are a few explanations for some decorating products you might encounter in this book. Most edible toppings are made primarily from sugar and cornstarch.

Cupcake Picks: Usually made of plastic or paper, these are small, non-edible decorative or themed icons on sticks for piercing into the tops of cupcakes.

Dragées and Pearls: Edible hard metallic and colored balls that range in scale from 2 to 8 millimeters, and larger. Not for children 3 and under.

Fondant and Gum Paste: Two varieties of sweet dough that can be rolled and/or molded into decorations, such as flowers or small sculptures. Technically edible, though not tasty.

Glitter, Disco Dust, and Twinkle Dust: Edible sparkly, metallic sugar confection ranging from extremely fine "dust" to fine "glitter."

PRO-TIP: To avoid a sparkle-covered kitchen, drill three tiny holes in the lid of an edible glitter container.

Royal Icing Decorations: Sweet icing piped into decorations, such as flowers. Dries very hard; technically edible, though not recommended.

Jimmies (Sprinkles): Classic oblong bakery sprinkles with a softer texture.

Nonpareils (called "Hundreds and Thousands" in the UK): Crunchy, tiny, colored balls.

Quins: Colorful candy sprinkles in small shapes like flowers, hearts, stars, and circles with a hard, crunchy texture.

Petal, Pearl, or Luster Dust: Superfine dust in an array of colors used to "paint" edible flowers and decorations. Also works to tint buttercream in a pinch. Use a small paintbrush and gold luster dust to create gilded berry toppers.

Sanding Sugar: Clear or colored sugar in slightly larger granules than regular tabletop sugar that has a natural "sparkle." Comes in regular and coarse.

HOW TO EDGE A CUPCAKE: Place a cup of your sprinkles of choice in a small bowl. Scoop up a generous amount of sprinkles in your nondominant hand. With your other hand, gently pick up your cupcake by the liner. Carefully dip the edges of the frosted cupcake in the pile of sprinkles in your hand, rotating the cupcake until you have covered the edge all the way around.

Sugar Toppers: Any form of edible decoration made primarily from sugar, sometimes called molded sugar toppers.

Wafer Paper: Light, edible sheets and decorations (flowers and leaves) that look like paper.

(I love custom ones!), gum paste flowers, sugar toppers, and good old-fashioned sprinkles. FancyFlours.com offers a good selection. Stock your pantry with an array of accoutrements so you'll be able to create every type of effect under the sun—from swank to sweet.

Now on to tints! Stock your pantry with a rainbow of gel or paste food colorings, which I find work the best to tint buttercream. Ateco makes a great twelve-pack (available at WebstaurantStore.com). I also love natural tints, which differ from gels in that they're made with colorants from edible plants (available at IndiaTree.com). However, they're much trickier to use: it's difficult (sometimes downright impossible) to get perfect saturation of some hues. With an array of great colors in your pantry, you can tint buttercream to the exact shade you need for your party, or tint your own sanding sugar (see page 33).

Trophy Frosting Techniques

Hand-Frosting. If you've made cupcakes before, you're probably well versed in frosting by hand. Hand-frosting is simply placing buttercream on a cupcake and covering the surface with a butter knife or, ideally, an offset spatula. At Trophy, we especially love three kinds of hand-frosting: domed, flat, and freestyle.

- **Domed frosting** looks exactly like it sounds: a perfect dome of buttercream atop a cupcake. Start by placing a 1½-ounce scoop (or your desired amount of buttercream) on top of the cupcake. Using an offset spatula, start in the center of the buttercream and "pull" it down to the edges of the cake. Use the spatula to cover the top of the cake in buttercream. The goal is to keep the center high and create a perfectly smooth, mushroom cap–like effect on top. For a super smooth surface, drag the offset spatula across the buttercream very lightly.
- **Flat frosting** is for whenever a canvas is required for writing a message, such as "Happy Birthday" or "World's Best Mom." A flat surface is also good for piping intricate characters or designs. To hand-frost a flat-style cupcake, scoop the desired amount of buttercream onto the cupcake. Use an offset spatula to flatten the top and drag the buttercream down the *sides* of the cupcake. The goal is to create an extremely smooth flat top and vertical sides.
- **Freestyle frosting** is a term that incorporates a variety of creative styles that are a variation of the domed style, such as waves for a beach party, elegant swirls for a wedding. Simply place the desired amount of buttercream on your cupcake and frost following the "domed frosting" directions above, then get creative making textures in the buttercream. Try figure eights, Cs, zigzags, and dips and pulls until you achieve the texture you desire.

PRO-TIP

Visit the Video section of TrophyCupcakes.com/book to see these techniques in action.

Rolled Frosting. This is our favorite technique! Rolling is quite simple but will have your guests thinking you spent days perfecting your gorgeous cupcakes. Basically, you dunk each buttercream-topped cupcake into a bowl of the topping of your choice (sprinkles, mini chocolate chips, shaved coconut, chopped nuts, mini candies, etc.) and roll it around to make a dome.

Start by filling a medium mixing bowl half full with the topping of your choice. Use a 1½-ounce scoop to place buttercream on the center of each cupcake. Now this is the part that scares people: *gently* hold the cupcake by its liner, turn it upside down and smoosh it gently (buttercream side down) into the topping. Don't push too hard, but apply a little pressure so the buttercream starts to squish towards the outer edges of the cake. Now gently rock the cupcake to the left, pushing the buttercream down closer to the edge of the cake, then rotate the cupcake and rock it again to the left, repeating until you've pushed the buttercream evenly over the entire cupcake. If your dome is not quite perfect, gently pat the sides and top of the cupcakes (with a super clean or gloved hand) to smooth out the sprinkles and shape. You should now have a perfect dome of yummy, coated buttercream!

TINT YOUR OWN SANDING SUGAR AND COCONUT FLAKES

If you love using sparkly sanding sugar as much as I do, or if you have a hard time finding just the right color, you'll want to buy a large box of clear sanding sugar and tint your own custom colors. It's super easy and much less expensive than buying small bottles of every color you want. We tint custom colors all the time, to match swatches provided by brides-to-be or the specific hues called for by a color-themed party.

- Place 1 cup of clear sanding sugar in a gallon-size plastic resealable bag and squeeze in 1 or 2 drops of gel food coloring. Seal the bag and knead it until the color is evenly distributed through the sugar. If the color isn't dark enough, add another drop. However, the color will deepen as the sanding sugar dries, so stop adding food coloring when the color is just a bit lighter than what you ultimately want.
- Pour the sugar onto a cookie sheet lined with parchment or wax paper. When it's dry, pour it into an airtight container. Once you have a rainbow of colors in your pantry, you can blend them to create any color combination you can dream up.

NOTE: These same directions apply to coconut flakes.

Piped Frosting. Basic piping skills are easy to master—trust me!—and only require a couple of pastry tips and a steady hand. What follows are the same techniques we use at Trophy to make classically beautiful cupcakes: Basic Swirl, Trophy Wave, Vintage Ruffle, Poppy Flower, and Writing. Once you master these techniques, you can attempt more-complex and detailed patterns and invest in elaborate pastry tips. But for now, I'll stick with the basics.

2
1
8
7

3
4
5
6
1. Vintage Ruffle
2. Basic Swirl — round tip
3. Hand-Frosted — dome
4. Trophy Wave
5. Poppy Flower
6. Basic Swirl — star tip
7. Rolled Frosting
8. Hand Frosted — freestyle

How to Fill a Pastry Bag

- First, choose the right tip for your preferred piping style (I include tip numbers with the instructions for each technique) and place it in your bag so it faces out through the small hole at the end. Cuff the open end of the bag over your hand. Using a spatula, fill the bag halfway with buttercream.
- Next, unfold the cuff and twist the top of the bag with a nice, tight twist, so frosting doesn't come out of the top while you're decorating. You can also secure the twisted top with a rubber band or twist tie. I recommend "massaging" the bag lightly to work out any air bubbles in the buttercream before twisting the top.
- For children, use a smaller bag and secure the top above the buttercream with a rubber band to prevent messes. (This makes piping much easier for little hands.)

How to Hold a Pastry Bag

Curl your fingers around the bag, placing the twist between your thumb and index finger. This forces the icing down into the tip each time you squeeze. Apply even pressure with all four fingers; the icing will come out of the tip until you stop squeezing. As you decorate, periodically twist the bag to force the icing down into the tip. Use the fingers of your other hand to guide the tip as you decorate. When your pastry bag is empty, simply untwist it, fold the cuff down, and refill.

PRO-TIP

Don't overfill the pastry bag: you'll have less control over the output and risk the mess of buttercream spurting out of the top.

Be a Piping Pro

Basic piping does take a bit of practice, but I'm betting you'll master it quickly! Keep these tips in mind:

- Hold and squeeze the bag with the hand you write with, and use your other hand as a guide.
- Hold the bag straight up and down (at a 90-degree angle from the surface) for Basic Swirl and Trophy Wave styles, and at a 45-degree angle for Vintage Ruffle and Poppy Flower styles.
- Use firm, even pressure when squeezing the bag.
- Hold the tip slightly above the cupcake surface while piping—don't drag the tip through the buttercream.
- To create a perfect little point on the top of the swirl, release pressure and pull quickly away from the cupcake.

Basic Swirl. A large round tip creates a basic swirl of buttercream; we use Ateco tip #809. A large closed or open star tip (also called a French tip) creates a basic swirl with lined grooves; for buttercream we use Ateco tip #828 (for both low and high swirls) and for our meringue frosting we use Ateco tip #867. Decide which effect you'd like and insert a large round or star tip into the pastry bag, then fill the bag halfway with buttercream or meringue.

Hold the bag at a 90-degree angle and aim the tip at the center of the cupcake (this helps hide the "tail" of the frosting—you'll see what I mean when you start!). Begin piping the frosting from the center, out to the edge of the cupcake, then around in a circle. For a low swirl of buttercream, pipe the frosting around the cupcake once, then without stopping, go back to the center and make a little point as you pull up (see Be a Piping Pro, page 36). For a high swirl—imagine a soft-serve ice cream cone—pipe two or more layers of swirls. Be sure to make the swirls smaller as you work toward the center. Again, finish in the center by pulling up to create a nice point of frosting.

Trophy Wave. Our signature Trophy Wave is really a hybrid of a classic swirl. Start by filling a pastry bag fitted with an Ateco #847 closed star tip. Hold the bag at a 90-degree angle and aim the tip ½ inch from the outer perimeter and start piping a swirl. Go out to the edge six times, then back in, while going around the whole cupcake. When the buttercream connects and you've made six "points," finish by moving your tip to the center of the cupcake and making a small swirl to cover the center of the cake.

Vintage Ruffle. You can re-create our signature ruffled frosting by using Ateco petal tip #127. Fill your pastry bag halfway (or even less) for maximum control. Hold the bag at a 45-degree angle and aim the tip about 1 inch from the outer edge of the cupcake (with the thick end of the tip closest to the cake). The buttercream will be piped from the perimeter in toward the center, creating overlapping ruffles. Squeeze the bag while simultaneously rotating the cupcake with your other hand, to form ruffles. With each rotation, move the pastry tip toward the center of the cupcake; squeeze harder for more pronounced ruffles.

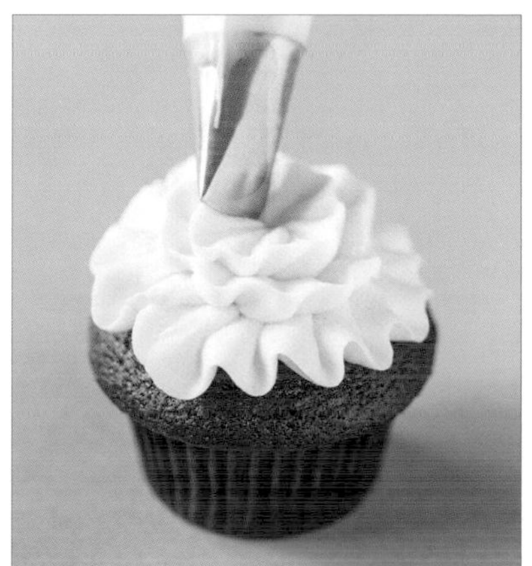

Poppy Flower. It's super easy to turn a Vintage Ruffle into a Poppy Flower design. Follow the instructions for the Vintage Ruffle, then simply pipe a dollop of frosting in the very center using a large round tip.

Writing. It's thoughtful to write sweet salutations such as "Congratulations!" on cupcakes, and we like to use Ateco tip #2 or #4 for messages of endearment.

Be sure to hand-frost your cupcake in the flat style (see Trophy Frosting Techniques, page 32), although a dome will work for shorter messages. When you're ready to write on your cupcakes, if you're feeling confident, go freehand. Otherwise, use a toothpick or a wooden skewer to lightly write what you'd like in the flat buttercream, then trace the lines with the piped buttercream.

To get started, hold your pastry bag at a 45-degree angle and touch the tip to the frosting surface. Squeeze at your starting point so the icing sticks to the frosted cupcake. Now raise the tip slightly and, as you squeeze, guide it just above the surface. To stop writing, stop squeezing and touch the tip to the surface, then pull it away. If your icing ripples, you're squeezing too hard. If it breaks, you're moving the bag too quickly.

Even basic writing takes practice, so keep these tips in mind:

- Use a small (10- or 12-inch) pastry bag and fill it just one-half full.
- Make sure your buttercream is room temperature. Cold buttercream will not pipe as easily.
- Practice on parchment paper before you work on the cupcake. To make a practice template, trace several 2½-inch circles (use a circle template from a craft store or a

2½-inch-diameter drinking glass) on regular paper with a dark black pen. Lay parchment paper over the paper, and practice writing your desired message *within* the circles. You can also practice fancy scripts using this same template method. Buy a handwriting book or open a magazine to a fancy script you like, then lay the parchment over the paper and trace it until you've got it. For this template, we printed out "Happy Birthday" (using the free font Black Jack, available at DaFont.com/Black-Jack.font) within 2½-inch circles, then laid parchment paper over that to practice.

- When you're done, scrape the practice buttercream back into your bowl using an offset spatula.

When it comes to piping (and pretty much every other artistic endeavor), practice makes perfect. So have fun, be patient, and relax, knowing that your family and friends are going to adore your homemade cupcakes.

More About Trophy Cupcakes

Our philosophy on buttercream is that "too much buttercream" is an oxymoron. *Really* good buttercream is the stuff of gods—light, creamy, melt-in-your-mouth dreaminess.

One of the things that make cupcakes so utterly amazing is the cake-to-frosting ratio. In our minds, if your cupcake is assembled correctly (and you eat it creatively), you should get a generous bite of creamy buttercream in each mouthful. Therefore, the recipes in this book will yield enough buttercream for a *very* generous swirl on each cupcake.

That said, some people prefer less buttercream. If you're one of them, simply halve the recipes or use the extra buttercream for another project (whoopie pie filling, cream-filled cookies, or whatever you dream up). Or store the excess in the refrigerator for up to a week when inspiration may strike again.

PRO-TIP

Some cupcakes have a delicious secret inside: filling! Make a yummy cupcake even yummier by filling it with buttercream, jam, lemon curd, or a specialty filling. See page 179 to learn how.

SPARKLE, COLOR & PATTERN

Great party planners have a very well-kept secret: you don't need to go all out and develop a super-complicated or obscure theme to make your event impressive and memorable. While I adore detailed, thematic parties based around people, places, or things, I also embrace celebrations centered on a simple concept. And you'll be amazed how basic elements can create an absolutely gorgeous party space.

In this chapter, I'll show you how a palette based on sparkle, color, or pattern can take center stage so that your food and drink, games, music, and entertainment can be anything you wish. I especially love this theme for landmark events such as anniversaries, weddings, engagements, and birthdays—where the spotlight is on the guest (or guests) of honor, but the hostess still wants to create a phenomenal, eye-catching environment.

You can apply this concept to any style of party and create a scene that will wow guests. Imagine the possibilities: a tartan-themed event for a Scottish family reunion; a rainbow-glitter party for a color-obsessed little girl; a baby's birthday marked by hundreds of festive polka dots; a "Louboutin red" or "Burberry plaid" fashionista celebration; or a "Think Pink" blowout, à la Audrey Hepburn in *Funny Face*. This easy concept is a great way to achieve maximum visual impact with the least amount of effort—so long as you shamelessly saturate every conceivable party element with your chosen sparkle, color, or pattern.

SPARKLE: ENGAGEMENT PARTY

Sparkle? Yes, sparkle! This kind of party is all about texture—and the texture in question is glittery, shimmery, twinkling sparkles. The Sparkle theme is a stunner for very special occasions, including New Year's Eve, milestone birthday celebrations, and engagement parties. I also love it for holiday galas and glitzy Hollywood awards show parties.

You're probably envisioning gold, silver, and bronze. But you'll be surprised how many metallic colors are out there, just waiting for you. Host a Pink Sparkle Party for someone's Sweet 16. Throw a Glittering Green Party for St. Patrick's Day. Or host a Winter Holiday Sparkle Party with twinkling lights and glittery snowflakes everywhere. Whatever color sparkle you choose, it'll look amazing when you use it throughout your event space.

For the engagement party that follows, I chose gold, a color that evokes the golden fiftieth wedding anniversary—a romantic goal to strive toward—as well as permanence, elegance, and glamour. Cocktail parties are fun to plan because they are the epitome of chic and classic style, place all of the attention on socializing, and give guests the opportunity to step out in style. Pair cocktails with all things sparkly, and you've created a gorgeous, effortless celebration.

SET THE STAGE

Go for Color

- Gold is positively gorgeous paired with pale pinks and champagne tones. If you choose silver, consider adding a stark white accent tone.

Decorate

- An engagement party is a celebration of years to come, so the invitation should feel classic and timeless but also reflect the tastes of the soon-to-be Mr. and Mrs. For this party, I worked with a letterpress designer to create a gorgeous invitation with gold "confetti" accents and a glitter-lined envelope. Guests will surely know that this party is of the ooh-la-la variety—a fun, celebratory bash.

DRESS YOUR GUESTS

For adult parties, it's nice to suggest attire. For fancier parties, or if you really want your guests to dress to specific guidelines, skip clever-yet-vague suggestions like "Dress to impress," and instead specify a traditional dress code such as "Semiformal attire" or "Black tie." However, I personally love weaving in wording like "Come in dance-party chic" or "Dress sparkly" because fun descriptions help guests get creative and start imagining the fun they are going to have. For the Sparkle: Engagement Party invitation I suggest writing, "Fine party frocks and dapper duds encouraged—especially if they're gold!"

Don't forget to mention attire for casual theme parties too. "Western-Wear Hoedown," "Don your shades and aqua pool attire," and "Dress Team Zissou" are all examples of suggestions that will get guests excited for the party well before the big day.

If you prefer to send electronic invitations, I love Kate Spade's "Come Celebrate" in gold on ivory, available at PaperlessPost.com.

- Your goal for the event space: sparkle, sparkle, sparkle. Clear balloons are a party planner's secret weapon because they add sparkle in a fun and elegant way without overpowering the rest of the decor. So fill your party space with countless clear, helium-filled balloons. Use them in copious amounts for huge, sparkly impact. I partially filled my balloons with gold glitter and confetti and tied them with beautiful gold strings. To fill balloons with glitter or confetti, you'll need a friend to help. One person holds the mouth of the (un-inflated) balloon open by inserting their pointer fingers into the balloon and stretching it wide. The other person can pour (or stuff) the desired amount of glitter or confetti into the balloon. Then fill with helium as usual.

- Dress round cocktail tables and the buffet table with champagne-colored table linens and shimmering gold table overlays. Then add gold chargers, gold or bronze flatware, and gold napkins (many rental companies can provide these metallic-toned items, as well as tables). Order lots of white or soft pink floral arrangements (or make your own) and place them in gold glitter vases (see Get Crafty, page 46). Purchase hundreds of ornamental gold paillettes in different sizes—I love the extra-large style—from a fabric shop and scatter them over tabletops as oversize confetti. If you use lots of paillettes, you may want to skip the gold overlays and chargers. When it comes to gold, think elegant, not overboard.

FROM FANCY TO FRUGAL: MY TOP 5 BUBBLIES

- Perrier-Jouët Fleur de Champagne Cuvée Belle Epoque
- Maison Bertrand Ambroise Crémant de Bourgogne NV
- Raventós i Blanc de Nit Cava Brut Rosé
- La Marca Prosecco DOC Extra Dry
- Francis Ford Coppola Sofia Blanc de Blancs (sometimes you just need the convenience of bubbly in a can!)

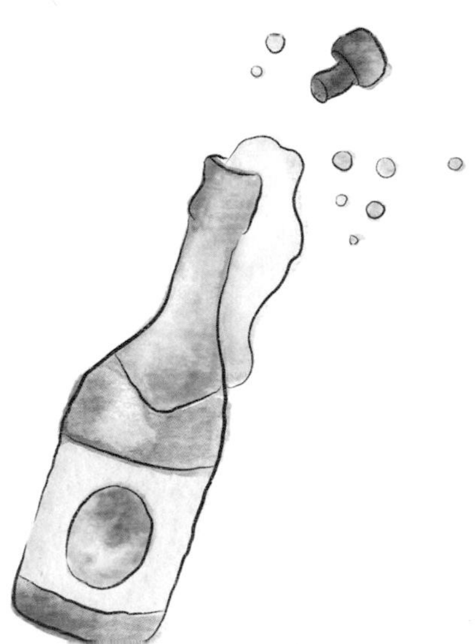

GET CRAFTY

Glitter Vases or Votives

Glam up your party's decor with glittery vases and candleholders. Head for a store that sells glass vases: you're looking for plain, sleek, clear cylinders in whatever size works for your arrangements.

SUPPLIES

- Kraft paper
- Masking tape
- Glass vases and/or votive candleholders
- Foam paintbrush
- Elmer's glue
- Thick-textured glitter (the thicker, the better), such as German glass glitter

1. Cover your work surface with kraft paper.
2. Using masking tape, mask off the top third of each vase. Using a foam paintbrush, cover the bottom two-thirds of the vase with a *very* heavy coat of Elmer's glue. (You want it to be quite thick so you get a very heavy coat of glitter on the outside.)
3. Pour the glitter over the glue until you have an even coat from the bottom of the masked area to the bottom of the vase. Set the vase aside to dry. When it's dry, carefully remove the tape for a very chic glitter vase. You can use this same technique for votive candleholders.
4. A nice way to tie in the glitter vases with your floral arrangements is to insert vintage-style millinery flowers (available online or, if you're lucky enough, at yard sales and antique stores) after edging them in the same glitter. (You could also experiment by spray-painting them gold.) Simply nestle the paper flowers carefully into your floral arrangements.

ENTERTAIN THEM

- Parties celebrating unions—anniversaries, weddings, and engagements—require a slightly more detailed version of the Truly Terrific Theme Generator (page 9). Ask the couple of honor where they met, what songs they fell in love to, their favorite music to listen to together, the best concert they ever saw together, and their all-time favorite movie.
- Use this information to create a playlist of their favorite love songs. Or better yet, give the list to a DJ and have him or her guide the spirit of the evening, using the song list as inspiration. Partnered guests may want to take a spin around the dance floor, so make sure your space has lots of room to move. Be sure to include an honorary champagne toast (see Toasting Tips, page 21).

HOW TO CREATE SIGNATURE COCKTAILS

Creating a signature drink beyond straightforward beer and wine is a brilliant way to add a special touch to a party and eliminates the need to host a fully stocked bar. (Not that I'd ever discourage you from providing both!)

For a lovey-dovey affair (such as a wedding, engagement party, or rehearsal dinner), it's marvelous to offer two signature cocktails: one to represent each partner. First, think about each person's favorite drink. Maybe it's a French 75 or a manhattan or a cosmo. Then think about putting a twist on each cocktail. It could be a flavor component, a clever name, or an ingredient that pays homage to a special place. How about a Huckleberry Kir in honor of a girl from Montana? Or a Bee's Knees to celebrate love with honey and ginger flavors? Or renaming a passionfruit caipirinha a Passionate Kiss? If you'd rather offer just one signature cocktail, you could play off the party theme, a combination of the couple's favorite cocktails, or the event's color palette. Maybe the glitter-rimmed champagne is dubbed the Mr. & Mrs. Glitterati! No matter what signature cocktail you choose to serve, it's guaranteed to make your event more memorable.

- To ensure even more great memories, set up a video, photo, or flip-book booth for tributes to the happy couple. Flip books—those little books that work like a mini movie when "flipped" through—are one of my favorite things of all time, and now there are companies that will come to your party and make them on demand with a photo booth! You can even customize the front and back covers. They're definitely among the cutest and most entertaining gifts I can think of. Make sure to have the vendor print out extras so the happy couple can take home a full set as a fun keepsake.

- Don't forget to make a festive backdrop for your video/photo/flip-book booth that matches your theme. I used a gold backdrop, tissue fringe garland (see page 116, directions 1 through 4), glitter-filled balloons, and a big basket of confetti that guests could throw in the air during their shots. Props are also essential; they help guests loosen up in front of the camera and send the fun factor soaring. Always try to provide props that match the theme of your party. For this one, we made gold glitter hearts and "X's" and "O's" on sticks, sparkly red lips, and provided large (but light) gold picture frames for guests to peek through.

SERVE UP BITES & SIPS

- Cocktail parties deserve fancy appetizers, such as oysters with Mignonette Sauce (page 75); Spicy Crab Toasts (page 142); figs filled with cheese, walnuts, and honey; spiced nuts (see page 49); endive leaves filled with pecans, blue cheese, and balsamic vinegar; and, of course, caviar.

- Unless you have lots of helping hands, you might consider hiring a caterer for such a special event. Waitstaff will make quick work of serving delicious nibbles to the crowd all night long, and you can also provide a bartender and full bar—so you can focus on enjoying the party!

- Bubbly drinks are a must. Why not serve champagne sprinkled with edible gold dust? Or, better yet, adorn the rim of each glass in edible gold glitter (this will result in glittery lips, so either be a little gauche and serve with a straw or only adorn one side of the rim).
- Also, don't forget to have some fun sips out for the kiddos. A maraschino cherry in anything fizzy will do the trick—but why not use the same tips in How to Create Signature Cocktails (see left) to create a nonalcoholic signature sip for the kids and teetotalers?

PRO-TIP

Swizzle sticks and drink picks are a fun way to adorn your signature cocktail and tie into your theme.

Sweet Al's Spiced Nut Mix

My good friend Alan Davis is an amazing chef and proprietor of Scout Provisions, a catering company in Seattle. His Spiced Nut Mix is the best I've ever had, and it's a wonderful addition to just about any party. It also makes a great parting gift for guests or a fun hostess gift. Thanks for sharing your recipe with us, Al!

MAKES 20 SERVINGS

1 cup each: almonds, walnuts, pecans, cashews, hazelnuts, and brazil nuts

1 cup olive oil, divided

1½ cups confectioners' sugar

1 tablespoon ground cumin

2 teaspoons ground cinnamon

1 teaspoon ground coriander

1 tablespoon finely chopped fresh rosemary

1 teaspoon fresh ground black pepper

- Preheat the oven to 325 degrees F.
- In a large mixing bowl, toss all the nuts with ½ cup of the olive oil.
- In a separate bowl, sift together the sugar, cumin, cinnamon, and coriander. Add the rosemary and black pepper, and whisk until incorporated.
- Add half of the sugar mixture to the nuts and toss to incorporate, using a wooden spoon. Add the remaining sugar mixture and toss to incorporate. Finally add the remaining ½ cup olive oil a bit at a time to ensure the oil and spices are coating evenly.
- Onto baking sheets lined with parchment paper, pour nut mixture in even single layers, using wooden spoon.
- Roast the nuts for 30 to 45 minutes. Every 10 minutes use the spoon to gently stir the nuts to ensure they are roasting evenly.
- When the nuts are uniformly golden brown, remove from the oven. Alan says "be sure to allow them cool before putting them in your mouth!"

GIVE THEM CUPCAKES

Pink Champagne Cupcakes

If you're lucky enough to have grown up with this classic special-occasion cake (or have a grandmother or neighborhood bakery that's kept the tradition alive), you know how wonderful this delicate pink treat is. It was extremely popular for weddings, bridal showers, and graduations in the 1950s and '60s, but it's grown harder and harder to find. Trophy serves it up every New Year's Eve and Valentine's Day; we like to think we're helping bring back a marvelous tradition.

MAKES 2 DOZEN CUPCAKES

What You Need:

- **Pink Champagne Cupcakes**, recipe on page 181
- 2 dozen metallic cupcake liners
- **Pink Champagne Buttercream**, recipe on page 197
- Gold edible glitter
- 2 dozen gold dragées

1. Bake the Pink Champagne Cupcakes in metallic liners of your choice, gold in this case, and pour yourself a glass (or two) of champagne while you're at it! If you're not drinking, note that one can of Sofia Blanc de Blancs is the perfect amount of champagne for this recipe.

2. While the cupcakes cool, make the Pink Champagne Buttercream.

3. Place the buttercream in a pastry bag fitted with a large star tip (we use Ateco #828) and pipe a generous swirl on each cupcake. Sprinkle with edible glitter and place a dragée in the center.

COLOR: AQUA POOL PARTY

There are endless shades in the color wheel, and you could create an amazing party theme around any one of them. Just pick your favorite color (or two or three) and . . . voilà! I zeroed in on aqua because it's dear to my heart. Aqua is one of Trophy's signature colors, and its soft cheerfulness has vintage and artistic qualities I just adore. The Aqua Pool Party theme works for a wide range of celebrations: favorites are fab bridal showers (maybe in Palm Springs!), summer birthdays, and even "Just 'Cause We Want to Throw a Party" parties.

SET THE STAGE

Go for Color

- Aqua, of course! And *lots* of it. For this pool party with a midcentury-modern twist, I paired as many aqua tones as possible.

Decorate

- If you're not lucky enough to have a pool in your backyard, find a local pool that allows parties or opt for a kiddie pool, sprinkler, or even a Slip'N Slide.
- Think Aqua Follies meets *Mad Men*, beginning with the invitation. Create an invitation on card stock featuring an aqua-and-white beach ball motif or a chic midcentury-modern pattern (see the Printables section of TrophyCupcakes.com/book). I also love the "Splish Splash" and "Bathing Beauties" e-invites from PaperlessPost.com for this party. Encourage guests to dress the part—in aqua bathing suits and sundresses, of course. Your party will look so chic, with guests wearing all shades of this delectable color!
- Stock the pool with umbrellas, towels, and all manner of toys and accessories in aqua shades. (Midcentury bar carts are a fun way to display the goodies.) Create seating areas of poolside tables and lawn furniture covered in aqua table coverings and cushions. Hang beach balls from tree branches as you would paper lanterns and make pennant garlands (see Get Crafty, page 53) to tie alongside.

GET CRAFTY

Pennant Garlands

Strings of pennant flags (also called bunting) are sweet and sentimental, evoking the happy spirit of old-school events. If you want the chic level to go through the roof, make your pennants with midcentury-modern patterned paper. Make loads of these and hang them everywhere. Don't be afraid to experiment with fabric or non-traditional shapes, like circles and squares.

SUPPLIES

- 1 sheet of 8½-by-11-inch white card stock
- Self-healing mat
- Utility knife
- 6 sheets of 8½-by-11-inch decorative card stock
- Pencil
- Ruler
- Bone folder (optional)
- 12 feet of ribbon or twine
- Invisible tape or washi tape (see page 20)

1. Using card stock, print out the pennant flag template, found on the Printables section of TrophyCupcakes.com/book. Lay the printout onto a self-healing mat and carefully cut it out using a knife.

2. Lay the decorative card stock right-side down and trace 2 pennant triangles onto the back of each sheet of paper. Cut out each pennant using the self-healing mat and knife.

3. With the paper right-side down, fold over the top of each flag about ½-inch. If you have a bone folder, run it across the fold to make it crisp. Carefully trim off the excess paper on the side of each pennant.

4. Run the ribbon or twine under the folded-down flap of the pennants, spacing them every 5 inches, and secure with tape. Use the extra length of ribbon on either end to hang the garland.

ENTERTAIN THEM

- Create a playlist of your favorite fun 1950s and '60s summery or beach-inspired songs to get your partygoers doing the cha-cha. (See How to Make a Playlist, page 14). Inexpensive portable record players are making a comeback and are easy to find online, in thrift shops, or in stores such as Urban Outfitters. The pop and crack of old vinyl creates a perfectly vintage lo-fi effect. Albums of surf music can often be found in bargain bins at your local thrift shop. Set up the player and records within earshot of the pool, and let guests have fun playing DJ.
- Set out aqua-colored baskets brimming with poolside necessities, including suntan lotion, misters filled with cooling cucumber water, pretty sarongs, and sunglasses

Wholesome Snow-Cone Syrup

MAKES 28 OUNCES

- Two 12-ounce bags frozen fruit, thawed, or 3 cups fresh fruit
- ½ cup agave syrup or superfine sugar
- Crushed or shaved ice

→ Place the fruit and agave syrup in a blender. Blend until very smooth. Strain through a mesh sieve to remove seeds and pour into a squeeze bottle or two, and chill. Squirt generously over crushed or shaved ice.

→ Make ahead! The syrup will keep in an airtight container in the refrigerator for up to a week or freezer for a month. Thaw before using.

→ Turn to page 57 for favorite syrup flavors.

(visit your local thrift store for wacky glam shades that'll have guests trying on every pair or, for a bridal shower, find inexpensive heart-shaped sunglasses).

→ It wouldn't be a pool party without plenty of water games! Organize bouts of Marco Polo, diving for pennies, a "Biggest Cannonball" contest, ring toss, and other favorite pool games. (For kids' parties, be sure to designate an adult or two to serve as lifeguards.) Your guests will play until they're wrinkled like prunes and have worked up an appetite. Of course, for grown-up parties such as a bridal shower, your guests may just want to don their biggest, most fabulous Hollywood shades and sip snow-cone cocktails while they lounge poolside.

→ Make several batches of Wholesome Snow-Cone Syrup (see recipe, above left) and package it in 8-ounce plastic squeeze bottles with custom labels, for a sweet parting gift. See the label template in the Printables section of TrophyCupcakes.com/book.

SERVE UP BITES & SIPS

→ At color-themed parties it's fun to offer a mix of colorful food (if your colors are appetizing, that is!). If adding the theme color to food doesn't quite feel right, stick with your favorite dishes, or the guest of honor's favorites.

→ For this aqua pool party, in lieu of blue food, I recommend serving 1950s and '60s summer favorites: shrimp cocktail, mini pigs in a blanket, deviled eggs, cheese balls covered in chopped nuts, a melon ball salad, and Jell-O—all served on aqua-colored platters, melamine plates, and vintage snack trays.

→ One place where blue foods work marvelously: treats! Using classic Jell-O molds feels very '50s and fun, so I made individual jiggly bites for kids, and grown-up versions spiked with good-quality vodka. The night before, you can also freeze aqua-hued drinks into popsicles that kids can cool off with.

→ Snow-cone machines are great—especially for making frozen cocktails—but I'm not a fan of imitation sugary syrup typically used as flavoring. So I concocted my own wholesome syrup (see recipe, above) for a delicious, all-natural version of this icy summery treat.

- Serve nonalcoholic aqua-hued sips in big aqua-colored drink tubs brimming with lots of ice, and don't forget blue-striped straws and paper umbrellas! I love Jic Jac Blue Raspberry and Jones Soda Berry Lemonade—both are the perfect hue for an Aqua Pool Party and sweetened with pure cane sugar. Jones Soda will even ship it to you with a custom label—imagine the guest of honor's face when she sees her photograph on the soda bottle!

GIVE THEM CUPCAKES

Snow-Cone Cupcakes

If you're looking to serve up some true eye candy, you can't beat these colorful cupcakes. Through the magic of food coloring, you can create nearly any color cupcake imaginable. Bake them in snow-cone cups for an utterly charming look—yes, I mean the actual paper cones made for serving the icy treats! It's a little tricky but makes for a very impressive presentation.

MAKES 2 DOZEN CUPCAKES

What You Need:

- **Vanilla Cupcakes**, recipe on page 182
- 2 dozen paper snow-cone cups (not waxed) and oven-safe holder, or 2 dozen 4-ounce soufflé cups
- **Vanilla Buttercream**, recipe on page 198
- Turquoise food coloring
- Coarse clear sanding sugar
- 2 dozen small wooden ice cream taster spoons

1. Bake the Vanilla Cupcakes in snow-cone cups. If you go this route, you'll need a metal snow cone or ice cream stand that is oven-safe, plus a cute way of displaying the cones once they're all decorated. If you can't find snow-cone cups, try 4-ounce white soufflé cups—great for baking cupcakes as they create an old-school, vintage look, plus you won't need cupcake pans. Simply place the soufflé cups directly on a cookie sheet. Keep in mind that soufflé cups do not peel off easily like a classic cupcake liner so you'll need to serve them with a small spoon.

2. While the cupcakes cool, make the Vanilla Buttercream.

3. Reserve a third of the buttercream in a separate bowl and set it aside.

4. Add 2 to 3 drops of the food coloring to the remaining buttercream and blend until you achieve your desired shade of aqua.

continued

5. Place the reserved buttercream and the aqua buttercream in separate pastry bags fitted with large round tips (we use Ateco #809).

6. Pipe one stripe of white buttercream down the center of half of your cupcakes. Then pipe a stripe of aqua on each side of the white. Alternate buttercream stripe colors on the remaining cupcakes. Use an offset spatula to pull the buttercream down the sides and create a smooth dome that stays high in the center. Be delicate and try to not disrupt the stripe pattern on the cupcake.

7. Coat entire surface of the buttercream in coarse sanding sugar, and garnish with a wooden spoon—or even a snow-cone straw/spoon!

Make Them Trophy

To make classic **Trophy Vanilla Vanilla Cupcakes**, place **Vanilla Buttercream** (page 198) in a pastry bag fitted with a large star tip (Ateco #828). Pipe a Trophy Wave (see Be a Piping Pro, page 36) on **Vanilla Cupcakes** (page 182) and sprinkle with **rainbow sanding sugar**.

FAVORITE SNOW-CONE SYRUP FLAVORS

- Blueberry-Basil (add 5 large fresh basil leaves to the ingredients in Wholesome Snow-Cone Syrup, page 54)
- Peach-Blackberry
- Orange-Peach
- Passion Fruit–Pineapple

FAVORITE ADULT SNOW-CONES

For the adults, stock a bar cart with your favorite cocktail makings. Encourage guests to pour two parts Wholesome Snow-Cone Syrup (page 54) to one part alcohol, over crushed or shaved ice for slushy grown-up treats.

- Blue-Basil Freeze (Blueberry-Basil Syrup with vodka)
- Hawaiian Snowflake (Passion Fruit–Pineapple Syrup with tequila)

oh baby!
KATE JAMES
Set the Stage — Shizen Patterned Paper
Get Crafty — Accordion Flowers
Entertain Them — Paint Pen Onesies
Serve Up Bites + Sips — Waffle Bar Brunch
Give Them Cupcakes — Lemon Meringue
Pie Cupcakes

PATTERN: BABY SHOWER

Here's another really fun and easy concept: base your party decor around a favorite pattern! Can you imagine how amazing a summer party would look swathed in gorgeous yellow gingham, or a graduation party saturated in an argyle pattern that matches the graduate's school colors, or a holiday party using your favorite candy cane striped wrapping paper? A Father's Day party could be a riot if the decor played off one of Dad's infamous garish tie patterns. This theme works for every type of party imaginable—in this case, a baby shower.

With patterns, the possibilities are endless. And just as with color, for achieving a truly terrific effect, the more pattern, the better. I find a lot of inspiration in creative wrapping papers and am a big fan of Snow & Graham (SnowandGraham.com), Smock (SmockPaper.com), Shizen Design (ShizenDesign.com), Rifle Paper Co. (RiflePaper.com), and Midori (www.Midori-Japan.co.jp/english). I fell in love with one of Shizen Design's adorable papers and created a baby shower around its pink, red, and orange scalloped pattern. This 100-percent recycled paper is handmade in India and has a sumptuous feel I can't get enough of.

SET THE STAGE

Go for Color

- There's no need to overthink this one—your color palette is determined by the pattern you choose. For this party, the colors are pink, red, orange, and, for a rich accent color, chocolate brown.

Decorate

- To get the full effect, you'll need lots of yardage of your pattern, whether it's paper or fabric, to cover adequate surface space and create crafts, decorations, and invitations.
- Set the stage for the theme with an invitation featuring your pattern. Using a template from the Printables section of TrophyCupcakes.com/book, cut a border from your featured pattern, whether paper or fabric, and paste it onto heavy card stock already printed with your party details. If your pattern is available in paper form, make matching envelopes using the pattern in the Printables section of TrophyCupcakes.com/book
- Of course, decorations are just begging to be made out of your pattern too. I used the paper to make a variety of Accordion Flowers (see Get Crafty, page 60) to hang around the party space.

- To create a "canvas" for your pattern to shine, cover a buffet in a plain tablecloth either in white or a coordinating color. Make a table runner by cutting a sheet of your patterned paper or fabric in half lengthwise, then connect the pieces end-to-end with double-stick tape. You can also cut circles 2 inches larger than your serving platters to create paper chargers. Line the tops of serving platters with your paper, if whatever you're serving is in packaging (such as cookies in cellophane or little nut cups filled with veggies or treats). Top it all off by using napkins, plates, glassware, and utensils in complementary colors pulled from your pattern. I used coordinating pink and orange napkins wrapped with napkin rings made by cutting 3-by-6-inch strips of the patterned paper and securing them with double-stick tape.

GET CRAFTY

Paper Accordion Flowers

Paper accordion flowers are classic and festive and very easy to craft. Make at least twelve flowers in varying large sizes to really wow your guests. If your paper is double-sided and you're hanging these flat on a wall, flip some to the alternate side for a twist. Or if you're using a patterned fabric, buy coordinating paper for your flowers or make Cloth Streamer Garlands instead (see page 74).

SUPPLIES

- 2 square pieces of paper per flower (two 12-inch squares will make a 12-inch flower)
- Scissors (if you're trimming edges)
- Permanent double-stick tape (or glue gun or stapler)
- Hole punch
- Ribbon or twine, for hanging

1. Take your 2 sheets of square paper and fold them accordion style (fan-fold) in 1-inch sections; smaller folds are appropriate for smaller flowers.

2. Round all 4 ends of the paper with your scissors to create a scalloped edge flower. You can also cut them into fun points or leave them uncut for a perfectly round and more modern-looking fan flower.

3. Fold each accordion-folded section in half, then unfold. Now place a strip of double-stick tape from the fold line to the end of the paper and refold, pressing hard to secure the 2 inner pieces of paper together and making a half-circle.

4. Place a piece of double-stick table along the inside edge of one of the half-circles, then secure the 2 half-circles together to make your round flower. Punch a hole near the top of your flower, secure the ribbon or twine, and hang.

♫ ENTERTAIN THEM

- You'll want to play background music, but don't feel like you need to stay within the bounds of "normal" baby shower music (i.e. songs with "baby," "sunshine," or "lovely" in the title). Find out what Mom's (or the parents-to-be) favorite songs are (check your Trophy-Worthy Party Planner, page 16) and create a playlist just for her.

- Lots of women love to play classic baby shower games. If your guest of honor is looking forward to that tradition, then by all means, indulge her. If not, there are lots of other options, such as crafty DIY projects, which are fun and sometimes practical too. My favorite such baby shower activity is Paint Pen Onesies.

PRO-TIP

Tiny Paper Accordion Flowers make great cupcake picks. Use 2-inch squares of paper, accordion-folded in ¼-inch sections, and place them on 6-inch skewers for cupcake picks made from your party pattern.

Paint Pen Onesies

- Cover a long table with butcher paper or a disposable tablecloth and place small buckets of nontoxic fabric paint pens or markers in the center. (Be sure to avoid glitter or small embellishments that could flake or pull off and become a choking hazard for baby.) Provide at least one plain onesie per party guest. I like white, but you can choose any color you like. Many stores sell them in packages (my favorite affordable brand is Gerber, which makes a four-pack of unisex organic onesies). I recommend buying three sizes—newborn, 3 to 6 months, and 6 to 12 months—so the parents (and baby) can enjoy them for the entire first year.

- Prewash the onesies, then fold them in neat stacks and place them in the center of the table on a pretty platter or cake plate. Place lots of stencils and decorative images around the table for inspiration, crank up the tunes, and let your guests go to town! String a clothesline nearby and have guests use clothespins to hang their finished onesies on the line to dry. (It looks super cute too!)

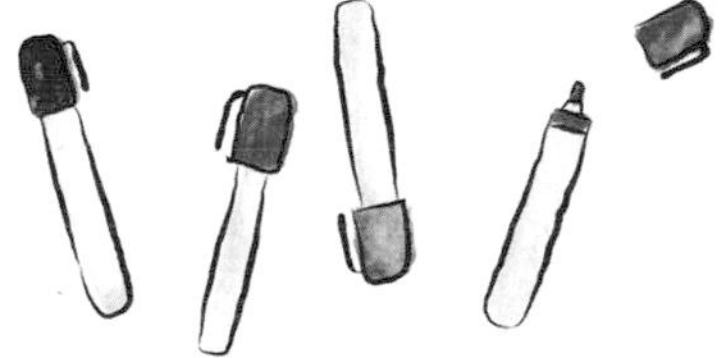

SERVE UP BITES & SIPS

- Don't worry: There's no need to serve patterned food! Instead, create a luscious spread of the guest of honor's favorite foods. This is a great opportunity to consult your Truly Terrific Theme Generator (page 9) and spoil the mommy-to-be (or parents to be) with all of her favorite foods. After all, she's eating for two, so forget about tea sandwiches and petits fours—unless that's what she's craving.
- Since most moms-to-be are exhausted by dinnertime, baby showers are best held in the morning or midday. For this reason, I like to throw brunch baby showers. Everyone loves a big spread of rich, sweet, or cheesy brunch items! If you don't have time to cook and bake up a storm (*mmmmm* . . . savory bacon-and-egg bread pudding, French toast, cinnamon-sugar doughnut holes, herb-roasted potatoes), create a fun and easy waffle bar, or find out where your guest of honor loves to go for breakfast or brunch. That restaurant might be able to cater your event.
- For brunch parties, I always like to set up a coffee and tea bar so guests can help themselves. A fresh juice and mimosa bar is nice too. Make things extra gorgeous by making swizzle sticks for the beverages using stir sticks and mini Paper Accordion Flowers (see Pro-Tip, below) made with your pattern.

PRO-TIP: Want to turn up the wow factor on your cupcakes? Cupcake wrappers/collars (decorative wrappers that you place on your cupcakes after baking) can be so much cuter than ordinary cupcake liners and really let you showcase your featured pattern. Use our template from the Printables section of TrophyCupcakes.com/book.

 GIVE THEM CUPCAKES

Lemon Meringue Pie Cupcakes

Moms-to-be often crave lemon and tart flavors—I know I certainly did when I was pregnant. This Lemon Meringue Pie Cupcake is a dream—whether you're expecting or not. Tangy lemon cake is filled with tart lemon curd so good, you'll want to eat it by the spoonful (or put it on waffles!). It's all topped off with fluffy, marshmallowy toasted meringue frosting. From preheat to first bite, these yummy cupcakes take at least four hours to prepare.

MAKES 2 DOZEN CUPCAKES

What You Need:

- **Lemon Curd**, recipe on page 213
- **Graham Cracker Crust**, recipe on page 216
- **Lemon Cupcakes**, recipe on page 183
- **Meringue Frosting**, recipe on page 199
- Apple corer
- Kitchen torch

1. First make the Lemon Curd.
2. While the lemon curd is chilling, make the Graham Cracker Crust.
3. While the crust cools, make the Lemon Cupcakes.
4. Fill the cupcake liners (with the graham cracker crusts in place) three-quarters full with the cupcake batter, and bake until the tops of the cupcakes are firm, and a cake tester inserted in the center of a middle cupcake comes out with just a few crumbs, about 20 minutes. Let the cupcakes cool for 5 minutes in the pans before removing to a rack to cool completely.
5. When the cupcakes are cool, core and fill each (see How to Fill a Cupcake, page 179) with a generous amount of lemon curd.
6. Make the Meringue Frosting. Immediately place it in a pastry bag fitted with a large star tip (Ateco #867) and pipe a triple swirl on each cupcake.
7. Using a kitchen torch, brown the meringue by lightly brushing the flame close to the meringue until it's brown (be careful not to get too close and burn or catch the meringue or the cupcakes liners on fire).
8. Serve immediately or within 2 hours.

PRO-TIP

To save time, make the graham cracker crust and the lemon curd at least a day in advance. See individual recipes for details.

COLOR: RED PARTY

Here's one more quick, simple color party idea to help you paint the town, well . . . red! Red is endlessly festive and makes for a great theme any time of year. Red is the color of love, rubies, and strawberries. And it's the color most associated with happiness in China. So choose your favorite shade of this hue and throw a red party!

SET THE STAGE

- Whether your shade of choice is cardinal, crimson, scarlet, or wine, blanket absolutely everything in red. Start with a red invitation and encourage your guests to dress in red (see Dress Your Guests, page 43). Next, decorate everything using red: balloons, crafts (see Get Crafty, below), and premade tissue paper decorations or crepe paper streamers. (Or all of the above!) This party is equally awesome for people who adore the color and Louboutin lovers, or for celebrations of American Heart Month and Valentine's Day.

GET CRAFTY

- Make your favorite decorations in red, such as Paper Accordion Flowers (page 60), Tissue Paper Pom-Poms (page 146), or Pennant Garlands (page 53), and hang them everywhere. Use wide rolls of red crepe paper as table runners—trim to fit your table size.

ENTERTAIN THEM

- For a color party, your entertainment should be inspired by the occasion. For example, a fun Valentine's Day activity would be a "DIY Valentine" craft table with lots of paper, doilies, heart craft punches, scissors, tape, and glitter pens. For a general red party, make a playlist with songs that feature red, such as: "Little Red Corvette" by Prince, "Red Red Wine" by UB40, "(The Angels Wanna Wear My) Red Shoes" by Elvis Costello, and "Red Rain" by The White Stripes. See how long it takes for your guests to realize the common thread!

SERVE UP BITES & SIPS

- Serve up yummy red-hued foods. Depending on the occasion and season, it could be pasta with red sauce; stuffed red peppers; a vibrant fruit tray with cherries, watermelon, raspberries, and strawberries; or maybe even steak tartare on toast. Don't forget red wine for adults and red sodas or cranberry juice for the kids.

GIVE THEM CUPCAKES

Red Velvet Cupcakes

Trophy's Red Velvet Cupcake is hands down our most popular flavor. People can't seem to get enough of this traditional Southern buttermilk cake with a hint of cocoa and cream cheese frosting. Maybe it's because it's red; maybe it's because of *Steel Magnolias*; or, in our case, the little red candy heart on top might be the culprit—regardless, it's a light and delicious cake that's perfect for any occasion.

MAKES 2 DOZEN CUPCAKES

What You Need:

Red Velvet Cupcakes, recipe on page 184

Cream Cheese Buttercream, recipe on page 200

2 dozen red candy hearts (optional)

1. First make the Red Velvet Cupcakes.
2. While the cupcakes cool, make the Cream Cheese Buttercream.
3. Place the buttercream in a pastry bag fitted with a large star tip (Ateco #828), and pipe a low swirl on each cupcake. Top with a red candy heart.

London Underground
KLASSE
SEATTLE TACOMA
EUROPA
CANADA
PERU

AWAY WE GO!

Travel is one of life's greatest pleasures. It's the ultimate escape—both a break from routine and a transformative gateway to new sights, smells, tastes, and people who are wonderfully unfamiliar. Everyone I know is in love with at least one location, whether it's a favorite international city or a special place that holds a personal memory.

Why not turn a great destination into a party, creating a festive celebration that captures that place's flavors, colors, sounds, and scenes? Imagine a party themed around colorful India, fashionable New York City, or even somewhere in the great outdoors, such as gorgeous Yellowstone National Park.

Once you've selected a place to celebrate, break out your Trophy-Worthy Party Planner (page 16) and start brainstorming how the various party elements can be infused into every detail. From the invitation and decor to the food and cupcakes, this chapter will help you explore ways to take a rich cultural journey without ever leaving home.

DESTINATION: PARIS

The City of Lights is one of those always-in-style party themes because, let's face it, it's Paris! You can have a lot of fun with this theme, going elegant and chic, or pink, cute, and whimsical. Some Paris-themed events that make me swoon: Bastille Day celebrations, bridal showers, and dinner parties.

Paris's markets are legendary. I often daydream about exploring their patisseries and *boulangeries*, eating every flavor of *macaron* and tart my stomach can hold, so I've whipped up a Paris party inspired by rue Cler, one of the city's most famous market streets. This cobblestoned lane is lined with vendors offering everything from escargot and caviar to fresh flowers and antiques, and its charming aesthetic translates easily to a casual French party. Focus on the simple love of food, drink, and company that Parisians savor, and draw on its beautiful details.

SET THE STAGE

Go for Color

- The French flag's navy, white, and crimson stripes make a perfect visual threesome. For a softer effect, use a muted version of these same three colors, plus a light peach accent.

Decorate

- Begin with café lights. Strings of classic round bulbs create a strong impact and can be repurposed later to spruce up your patio or add to holiday decor. Tie in the color palette by loosely weaving Cloth Streamer Garlands throughout the lights (see Get Crafty, page 74).
- To evoke the feel of a French market, use rustic stands or wooden produce (or wine) crates under platters of food atop an old wooden dining table. Stand extra "prop" baguettes in baskets or metal tins. Label cheeses with mini chalkboard signs. Create a quintessential Parisian café sign on a chalkboard—ours is a popular French saying, "Eat well, laugh often, love much."
- Never be afraid to be your own florist for casual parties among friends. Make your own herbes de Provence arrangements of thyme, lavender, rosemary, and savory, and place them around the party space in old bottles or vintage tea and coffee tins. Fill each "vase" with water, strip away any leaves resting below the waterline, and cut the herbs about the same height. A loose, casual arrangement is often the most appealing, so relax and embrace your inner florist!

Mangez Bien
Riez Souvent
Aimez Beaucoup
roquefort
epoisses berthaut
pain au levain
baguettes

legumes
de l'olive

GET CRAFTY

Cloth Streamer Garland

I love standard crepe paper, but to capture the old-world feel of this party, I decided to create hand-dyed cloth versions of classic streamers. Cloth streamers create a lovely vintage look, allow for a perfectly matched color palette, and are a great project to do with kids!

SUPPLIES

1 yard white 100 percent cotton fabric (or an old white cotton sheet); you'll get about 50 2-by-18-inch-wide strips of fabric per yard of 54-inch wide fabric.

Fabric dye, such as Rit Dye

Scissors

Ruler

12 feet of heavy twine

1. Several days before the party, wash and dry the fabric. This removes the sizing (if it's new fabric) and will help the fabric hold the dye better.

2. Dye the fabric following the manufacturer's instructions. To find the perfect color for your party, use Rit Dye's "ColoRit Color Formula Guide." It's awesome!

3. Dry the fabric in your dryer and promptly remove to avoid wrinkling. But there's no need to iron—we want the strips to look rustic.

4. Carefully rip the fabric into 2-inch strips that are 18 inches long. For 1 yard of fabric, fold the fabric in half lengthwise and make a ½-inch snip on the fold with scissors and carefully rip into two 18-inch sections, then make a small ½-inch snip every 2 inches down the length of each section and carefully rip into 2-inch strips. You'll need about 40 to 50 strips per 12 feet of garland, depending on how closely you'd like them spaced.

5. Tie the strips onto heavy twine about every 3 inches and voilà! You now have a cloth streamer garland in your exact party color. You can use the same method with long strips using the full length of the fabric (54 inches) to create cute cloth backdrop.

ENTERTAIN THEM

- This theme is perfect for celebrating good food, so let your mind go wild with various food-related activities (other than eating) you could share with your guests, such as a mustard- or preserves-making station or blind champagne and/or cheese tastings.
- Camaraderie and good-natured competition makes *pétanque*, a popular pastime in Paris parks, the perfect outdoor party game. For the kids, set up wine bottles on a low table for a fun ring toss game. Each time a ring makes it onto a bottle, offer up a fun French-themed prize such as a French flag temporary tattoo or a fake mustache

TOP 5 MUST-DO'S WHEN VISITING PARIS

- Rent an apartment. You will feel like a true Parisian as you leave your *appartement* to shop the local markets for snacks and wine to enjoy in the comfort of your own "home."
- Eat falafel in the Marais. Head to rue des Rosiers, a tiny cobblestoned street filled with fragrant falafel shops. My favorite is L'as du Fallafel, which, by the way, claims to be Lenny Kravitz's favorite Parisian falafel too.
- Watch the Eiffel Tower sparkle. Silly *moi*. I had no idea la Tour Eiffel now sparkles every hour, on the hour, once night falls. Sit along the river at the place de la Concorde and take in this pretty, dazzling, sparkling sight!
- Visit Pierre Hermé. Pierre Hermé is arguably the world's most famous chocolatier and pastry chef. Naturally, you must visit one of his seven pastry "boutiques" and purchase an assortment of *macarons*.
- Ride a riverboat at night. Yes, touristy boat tours can be cheesy, but not in Paris. Grab a bottle of wine and head to the Seine, where you can hop aboard a long boat that will drift past some of the city's most noteworthy landmarks.

sticker. For kids' parties, you could also provide red berets and lots of props to create a lighthearted French photo op.

- How about some music? Paris is about sights, smells, and tastes, but it's also about sounds. Buskers (outdoor musicians playing for pocket change) are seemingly on every street and subway, and the sounds of their old-world accordions, stand-up bass fiddles, violins, portable pianos, and Spanish guitars resonate long after you've returned home. To really bring Paris to your party, hire a local musician and chanteuse to serenade your guests, a classic three-piece to provide background cocktail music, or an upbeat chanson outfit that will get even the most timid guests dancing. If you prefer a playlist, download Putumayo's "Paris" or "French Café"—fun mixes for Francophiles.

SERVE UP BITES & SIPS

- Forget those notions about fussy French food. The most delicious French cuisine is the simplest of all! Baguettes, a spread of French cheeses (with at least one stinky cheese, such as Epoisse de Bourgogne or Roquefort—available at most gourmet grocers), olives such as picholine or Niçoise, pâtés, cornichons, Dijon mustard, fresh veggies, and

Mignonette Sauce

Combine **1 teaspoon crushed black pepper**, **1 tablespoon minced shallots**, and **2 tablespoons champagne vinegar**. Makes enough to accompany 1 dozen oysters. Store in an airtight container in the refrigerator for up to 3 days.

cured meats are really all you need. Visit your local specialty grocer or cheesemonger—I love DeLaurenti in Seattle—to help take your spread to the next level.

- The great thing about a rustic French buffet is that it's completely kid-friendly, so there's no need to make separate food for them. Baguettes with butter and ham or cheese and crunchy cucumbers, carrots, and haricots vert are a favorite among *les petits-enfants*.

French Soda

Fill an **8-ounce glass with ice**. Add **1 to 2 tablespoons of flavored natural syrup**. Slowly pour **club soda** over the ice (for a pretty layered effect), then add a splash of **half-and-half**, plus a **dollop of whipped cream** (if desired). Top it off with a striped mustache straw!

- If you're feeling ambitious, start the party with champagne and raw oysters served from an oyster station complete with an oyster shucker (ask a friend or poach a professional from your favorite fish monger or oyster bar for one night). Display the oysters on ice with lemon wedges and a bowl of Mignonette Sauce (page 75).

- It goes without saying that the bar must be stocked with good French wine and champagne. A Lillet Cooler (recipe, below) features the soothing flavors of mint and cucumber, and makes a delightful signature cocktail.

Lillet Cooler

1 cup ice, plus more for serving

½ cup Lillet Blanc

1 ounce vodka (Ketel One or your favorite)

2 tablespoons fresh lemonade

A few leaves of mint

Splash of soda water

1 cucumber spear and fresh mint sprig, for garnish

- Put the ice, Lillet, vodka, lemonade, and mint in a cocktail shaker and shake well.
- Fill a glass with ice; strain mixture into glass and add soda water.
- Garnish with cucumber spear and mint sprig.

PRO-TIP: You don't want to get stuck behind the bar all night, so for larger parties, make a large batch of Lillet Cooler. Just combine the first 5 ingredients (multiplied by how many you want on hand) in a pitcher or punch bowl alongside an ice bucket. Have the pitcher available to guests to pour over ice, top with soda, and garnish. Be sure to make a cute "Lillet Cooler" sign too!

- *Pour les enfants*, set up an ooh-la-la inducing French Soda bar with club soda, a variety of natural syrups (I like elderflower, lavender, and French vanilla for this party), half-and-half, and whipped cream (recipe on page 77).

GIVE THEM CUPCAKES

Lavender Crème Brûlée Cupcakes

Although crème brûlée's origins are hotly debated, it's quintessentially French to me and one of my all-time favorite desserts, so I just had to make it into a cupcake. It is a little trickier than Trophy's usual recipes, and you'll need some special equipment—at least ten 2½- to 3-inch metal biscuit cutters or mousse rings (straight-sided with no handle) and a kitchen torch. But the extra effort results in a most amazing creation: lavender-scented custard with a hardened-sugar crown atop our moist vanilla cupcake. *C'est magnifique!*

MAKES 10 CUPCAKES

What You Need:

- **Crème Brûlée Cupcakes**, recipe on page 185
- **Lavender Pastry Cream**, recipe on page 214
- Ten 2½- to 3-inch biscuit cutters or mousse rings
- Kitchen torch
- 10 teaspoons

1. Prepare the Crème Brûlée Cupcakes and the Lavender Pastry Cream, following the cupcake recipe's instructions for how to carefully assemble the two ingredients together, then bake.

2. Serve the cupcakes on a plate with a teaspoon so your guests can experience the ultimate pleasure of cracking the top. You can caramelize the tops up to 1 hour before you serve the cupcakes. Any longer than that, and the caramel will become watery.

PRO-TIP

For trickier recipes, do a test run a week or so prior to your event. Even experienced bakers can have trouble their first time with a recipe . . . and there's nothing worse than a failed attempt right before a party.

Set the Stage — Papel Picado
Get Crafty — Piñata
Entertain Them — Fiesta Music!
Serve Up Bites + Sips — Taco Bar
Give Them Cupcakes — Margarita Cupcakes

DESTINATION: MEXICO

Our neighbor to the south makes an ideal theme for so many types of events. There is Cinco de Mayo and Dia de los Muertos (Day of the Dead), of course, but festive Mexican music, crave-worthy food and drinks, brightly colored textiles, and the steamy, summery locale add a twist to lots of party styles, such as rehearsal dinners and summer soirees. Don't forget the margaritas!

SET THE STAGE

Go for Color

- Think juicy and bright hues—anything goes! Two of my favorite combinations are Kelly and light green with magenta and royal blue, and kraft-paper brown with papaya orange, magenta, and aqua accents.

Decorate

- To create a Mexican fete, start with tabletops. Colorful oilcloth is a traditional textile that comes in a huge variety of patterns and solids that range from tasteful to wild. You can find it at most fabric shops, and at OilclothbytheYard.com, "Animal Wonderland" is perfect for this party and resembles Otomí fabric. Otomí fabrics, made by the indigenous Otomí peoples, are embroidered with colorful, festive patterns that reflect the spirit of the Mexican highlands. Look for textiles that reflect your party palette. Mexican serape blankets (or serape-style tablecloths and runners) would be another great tabletop textile to brighten up your decor.
- Mexico also has a tradition of crafting amazing paper art that makes beautiful, affordable party decor. I love *papel picado*, perforated paper flag garland in an array of gorgeous hues that add bold pops of color to an event. For the invitation, there are many "Fiesta" e-invite options on PaperlessPost.com. However, "Fiesta Flags" and "Tulum," which feature papel picado imagery, are perfect for this party. Fresh flowers, such as dahlias, zinnias, marigolds, or carnations (in plain vases) with papel picado banderitas (paper flags on sticks) tucked in really amp up the salsa spirit.

PRO-TIP

For extra-special occasions and weddings, order customized papel picado with the theme or names of your choice!

- No Mexico-themed party is complete without a piñata. You can purchase one from a Latin market, find a local piñata artist to customize one for you, or make one at home (see Get Crafty, page 82). The homemade version makes a fun family activity in anticipation of the party.

GET CRAFTY

Homemade Piñata

A homemade papier-mâché piñata requires a little work (you'll need about four days, mostly unattended), but this unforgettable centerpiece is well worth the time.

SUPPLIES

- 14- to 16-inch perfectly round balloon
- 2 cups of all-purpose flour
- Water
- Newspaper, cut lengthwise into long strips about 1½ inches thick
- Sheets of colorful tissue paper, cut into fringed strips, or tissue festooning (available at craft and party stores)
- Glue stick
- Candy and/or prizes
- Thin rope or cord
- Blindfold (optional)

1. Inflate the balloon and place it on the mouth of a heavy drinking glass. (You may need to secure it with tape first.) Set aside.

2. Mix the flour with enough water to make a loose paste (not too thin or thick). Dip the newspaper strips into the paste and adhere them to the sides and top of the balloon, overlapping each strip in various directions. Flip the balloon over and cover the bottom. When the balloon is completely covered with strips of paper, let it dry overnight and repeat twice more for a total of three layers.

3. Once the three-layer surface is completely dry and hard, start on the tissue paper decoration, adhering the tissue with a glue stick to the bottom of the piñata and working your way toward the top. Overlap the tissue generously and only adhere the non-fringed sections of the tissue paper for a great textured effect. When the entire surface is covered in tissue and the glue is dry (about 2 hours), pop the balloon with a sharp implement. Then carefully cut a small hole or slit in the top of the piñata and fill the hollow with candy and/or prizes. Cover the opening with more tissue fringe if desired.

4. Punch two holes on either side of the opening and thread a thin rope or cord through the holes, leaving the ends long enough to suspend the piñata from a tree branch or ceiling hook. Now all you need is a big bat or stick, a blindfold, and someone to make sure everyone stands back!

PRO-TIP

For an over-the-top piñata, cut the tissue in scallops or diamond shapes, rather than fringed strips, and adhere them one at a time. Experiment with metallic paper or alternating colors.

♫ ENTERTAIN THEM

Breaking open a candy-filled piñata is the highlight of any fiesta—but don't forget the music and dancing. The following playlist is an upbeat collection of Latin American favorites that includes indie rock, Latin pop, Spanish guitar, and classic mariachi. Plug these tunes into your iPod and crank up the volume!

- Calexico, "Muleta" and "Tres Avisos"
- Manu Chao, "Mi Vida"
- Omara Portuondo, "Quizas, Quizas, Quizas"
- Orlando "Cachaíto" López, "Mis Dos Pequeñas"
- Bebel Gilberto, "Aganju"
- Buena Vista Social Club, "Chan Chan"
- Gloria Estefan, "Mi Buen Amor"
- Cesária Évora, "Petit Pays"
- Gipsy Kings, "Bamboleo"
- Manuel "Guajiro" Mirabal, "El Rincón Caliente"
- Ibrahim Ferrer, "Qué Bueno Baila Usted"
- Los Lobos, "Sabor a Mi"

My Favorite Lime Margarita

4 ounces silver tequila, such as Herradura Silver

1½ ounces freshly squeezed lime juice

1 ounce Cointreau

½ ounce Simple Syrup (recipe on page 85)

- Combine all ingredients in a cocktail shaker half full of crushed ice. Cover and shake well. Strain over ice-filled cocktail glasses with salted rims, if desired.

TWO FIESTA-FUN TWISTS:

- Ginger-Lime Margarita: Make **My Favorite Lime Margarita**, but pour it into a larger glass, top with 3 ounces ginger beer (try Rachel's if you are in Seattle, RachelsGingerBeer.com), and garnish with a **thin slice of fresh ginger root** and a **lime wedge.**
- Tangerine-Habanero Margarita: Make **My Favorite Lime Margarita**, but shake it with **3 ounces freshly squeezed tangerine juice** (orange juice will work in a pinch) and **1 or 2 very thin slices habanero pepper**. (Beware: Habaneros are one of the hottest chili peppers.)

SERVE UP BITES & SIPS

- Everyone knows that even the simplest Mexican food is delicious and can be very easy to prepare. A taco bar featuring all the fixings—beans, meats, salsas, guacamole, cheeses, sour cream, soft tortillas, and hard shells—will be a big hit with all ages and any type of group, especially picky eaters (who can make their own creations and be as selective as they like). Best of all, everything can be prepared in advance and placed on the table right before guests arrive. A tray of mini quesadillas can be prepped and toasted in less than half an hour, and a batch of gazpacho can be made a day or two in advance and served in shot glasses topped with fresh avocado. Arrange everything on beautiful Mexican *Talavera* plates or solid, color-coordinated serving pieces.

- Nonalcoholic *aguas frescas* are light, fresh-fruit punches that look pretty in punch bowls, glass pitchers, or large jars fitted with spigots. Jarritos is a brand of fruity, extra-carbonated soft drinks that are popular in Mexico and available in some U.S. grocery stores.

- Grown-up parties require a signature margarita with a fun twist that incorporates seasonal flavors—such as jalapeño, pureed watermelon, ginger, or grapefruit juice—or the guest of honor's favorite flavor. Be sure to give your signature drink a celebratory name, giving a nod to the guest of honor, of course.

Simple Syrup

To make your own simple syrup, simmer equal parts sugar and water until the sugar is dissolved. Cool. Then pour into a squeeze bottle (or pretty glass bottle with a nozzle) for a quick add to cocktails. Simple syrup will keep in the refrigerator for 2 weeks. It's also perfect for sweetening iced coffee and tea.

 **GIVE THEM CUPCAKES**

Margarita Cupcakes

I created this pre-Trophy cupcake, featuring a boozy tequila-lime buttercream and garnished with salt and lime, for my friend Heidi's birthday, which happens to fall on Cinco de Mayo. The fresh lime zest and juice along with the lime oil make for a refreshing citrusy flavor that'll make your guests shout "Tequila!"

MAKES 2 DOZEN CUPCAKES

What You Need:

Lime Cupcakes, recipe on page 187

Tequila Lime Buttercream, recipe on page 201

Clear sanding sugar

Margarita salt or *fleur de sel* (optional)

2 dozen pieces candied lime zest (recipe below) or small wedges from 2 fresh limes (optional)

1. Make the Lime Cupcakes.
2. While the cupcakes cool, make the Tequila Lime Buttercream.
3. Spoon the buttercream into a pastry bag fitted with a large round tip (Ateco #809).
4. Pipe a generous triple swirl on top of each cupcake.
5. Sprinkle with sanding sugar and margarita salt, then garnish with candied lime zest or a fresh lime wedge.

Candied Citrus Peel

2 organic limes (or other citrus)

1 cup sugar, plus more for coating

½ cup water

Channel knife or paring knife

- Peel limes and cut into ½-by-2-inch strips.
- Place peel in a small saucepan and cover with cold water. Bring to a boil, then drain and rinse with cold running water. Repeat process 2 more times, using fresh water.
- In a separate saucepan bring the sugar and water to a boil. Stir until the sugar dissolves, then add the blanched citrus peel. (If you are using larger fruits, double the sugar syrup or just use the peel from 1 fruit.)
- Bring syrup and peel to a boil and reduce heat to a simmer. Cook peel until tender and translucent in color, about 10 minutes. Remove from heat. Cool slightly, then remove peel with a slotted spoon or tongs. Lay peel on a wire rack to cool—placing a cookie sheet or parchment paper beneath the wire rack for easy cleanup—then toss in sugar until well coated. Transfer candied peel to an airtight container and store at room temperature for up to 1 month.

DESTINATION: HAWAII

Everyone who knows me knows that my personal destination obsession is the beach, and I love just about everything tropical. I have collections of shells, koa wood bowls, and dried leis all over my home. My dad was a surfer who made his own boards, and I spent the first year of my life on the beaches and in the water of San Diego. No doubt that's why a love of sun, sea, and sand has been in my blood from the start.

I didn't visit Hawaii until I was in my twenties, but once I arrived, I felt as if I'd been there before. The minute I smelled the intoxicating tropical flowers as I exited the plane, I knew it was the place for me. Is it any wonder that my husband proposed on Oahu's Waimanalo Beach (he arranged for an amazing picnic and then presented the ring inside a beautiful shell he "found") and that we eloped to Eva Parker Woods Cottage on the Big Island?

The Hawaii theme is fun for graduation parties, anniversary parties, and "Is It *Really* Still Winter?!" celebrations.

SET THE STAGE

Go for Color

- Nature and tropical flowers provide big-time inspiration here. My favorite color combinations are palm-tree greens, koa-wood brown, plumeria pink, and hibiscus yellow, or a simple pairing of white and brown, with plenty of shades of white tropical flowers and koa wood and kukui nuts.

MY TOP 5 FAVORITE THINGS IN OAHU

- Sunset mai tais at Halekulani hotel's House Without a Key
- Touring Shangri La, Doris Duke's breathtaking, Islamic-style estate built in 1937
- Chinatown's many, many lei shops
- Aloha Stadium Swap Meet & Marketplace, Hawaii's largest open-air flea market
- Watching big-wave surfing on the North Shore

Decorate

- Tropical flowers and foliage make a Hawaii Party pretty easy and absolutely gorgeous. Your invitation can be simple or very detailed (see Get Crafty, page 90). For the simple version, select a tropical/floral-themed invitation from a local shop or online stationary site (type in "Hawaii" on PaperlessPost.com for a great selection) and encourage guests to dress in island style.

- To embellish the party space, cut leaves from your yard's tropical plants if you have them or visit your local flower market (a wholesale flower market open to the public will more than likely have the best selection and prices). Look for big, brightly colored leaves and palm fronds to cover tables, line cake plates, and place in flower arrangements. If these sources aren't accessible, order flora online or create a stencil and cut out lots of oversize leaf shapes from pretty green paper.

- Flowers are a must: I love plumeria, tuberose, pikake, and white ginger. These beautiful, fragrant blossoms will instantly transport your guests to the islands. Orchids are stunning and sometimes easier to find; sprinkle loose ones everywhere, and place flower arrangements on every surface to bring the Aloha Spirit to your party.

- Present each guest with a fresh flower lei on arrival (vintage paper, shell, silk, or homemade leis are also lovely). Here in Seattle, we're lucky to have the Hawaii General Store & Gallery, an amazing shop where I pick up all my luau supplies, including fresh leis. If you don't have a store like this in your area, you can order fresh leis online from places like HawaiiFlowerLei.com.

- Leis also make incredible garlands: simply untie them, knot the ends, and hang different lengths of white leis over the food table from the ceiling or a tree branch, or string them together and hang them up as gorgeous floral garlands.

- To add sparkling light to evening parties, fill cylindrical glass hurricane lamps about one-third full of sand and top with votive or larger candles and a couple of small shells or a single orchid. Place a single candle on smaller tables and grouped candles on larger tables.

PRO-TIP

For kids, make candy leis by tying the ends of wrapped candy together with ribbon. For grads, make money leis!

GET CRAFTY

Lei Invitation

Whether it's created from beautiful paper, fragrant tropical flowers, or colorful candy, an exotic lei invitation will really wow your guests and get them excited about your event. Ancient Hawaiians believed that some leis provided protection and healing powers. Today, they're often given as a token of good luck. Giving someone a lei is a thoughtful, celebratory custom—and it makes the perfect invitation for a Hawaiian party.

SUPPLIES (PER INVITATION):

- Lei (handmade or purchased)
- Heavy paper
- Oval craft punch
- Hole punch
- ½ yard raffia or string

1. Make or purchase the lei of your choice.
2. Use the craft punch to create three ovals. Write your party details on them. Punch a small hole into each and attach all three to the lei using raffia. I like to use Hawaiian phrase like: *Ho'olu komo la kaua,* which means "Please join us."
3. Send or hand deliver each lei to the recipient in a small box.

ENTERTAIN THEM

- Hawaiian music will do a great job of setting the mood. Book an authentic Hawaiian band or create a Hawaiian playlist from iTunes, Pandora, or your favorite music site (see How to Make a Playlist, page 14). For fancier parties, consider hiring professional hula dancers to put on a truly memorable show for your guests.
- Hula or lei-making lessons are fun activities for both kids' parties and adult parties—especially a bridal shower or a Mother's Day gathering.

PRO-TIP

To make a crepe paper ti leaf lei like the one on page 91, go to the Video section of TrophyCupcakes.com/book.

SERVE UP BITES & SIPS

- Finger foods such as grilled shrimp, fish, chicken, and veggie skewers create a wonderful do-it-yourself buffet that's always a big hit. I love grilled pineapple as a delicious addition to skewers. Tropical fruit platters of mango, pineapple, coconut, and papaya are not only sweet but add to the decor. Order trays of ahi poke on taro crackers and sushi from your local sushi bar, or hire a sushi chef for the party. For a really special event, hire a caterer to create traditional luau fare, including a whole roasted pig!

Ho'olu komo la kana
May 14 2014
-6:30 PM-
dress island style

- Arrange the food on koa wood platters and bowls on a leaf-lined table, along with bamboo plates and utensils or clear glass serving pieces. Choose a wood or white table large enough for your buffet (or cover a long folding table with a brown or white tablecloth) and line the surface with large tropical leaves. Add beautiful flower arrangements and scatter loose orchid blossoms. Embellish platters and plates with simple, loose orchids.
- To me, there's almost nothing better than a cold fruity drink in hand, the smell of tropical flowers, and the sound of waves in the background—though the pleasant strum of a ukulele will suffice if you're not on the beach. Rather than stocking an entire bar, create one signature tropical drink (see How to Create Signature Cocktails, page 48) that is premixed and self-served, or have a bartender mix each drink individually. Have a few cases of Hawaiian beer—Longboard Lager from Kona Brewing Company or Big Swell IPA or CoCoNut PorTeR from Maui Brewing Co.—and chilled white wine or rosé, and your tiki bar is good to go.
- For kids' parties (or a nonalcoholic option at grown-up parties), create a tropical smoothie station where kids can choose their own fruits and juices and an adult does the blending.
- Every drink at a luau needs flair, so have plenty of garnishes on hand. I always say that a little paper umbrella paired with an orchid makes drinks taste so much better!

 GIVE THEM CUPCAKES

Piña Colada Cupcakes

Piña coladas are one of my favorite cocktails, and they taste especially decadent when served in a hollowed-out pineapple with a flower and a paper umbrella. But the flavors of coconut, rum, and pineapple taste good in any form, so creating a Piña Colada Cupcake was inevitable. If you want to avoid alcohol, omit the rum from the buttercream—this Pineapple Coconut cupcake will still be delicious.

MAKES 2 DOZEN CUPCAKES

What You Need:

Caramelized Pineapple, recipe on page 215

Vanilla Cupcakes, recipe on page 182

Coconut Rum Buttercream, recipe on page 202

½ cup toasted coconut (optional)

2 dozen maraschino cherries (optional)

2 dozen paper umbrellas (optional)

Crushed graham crackers (optional)

PRO-TIP

To create "sand," grind graham crackers in a food processor, or crush them inside a resealable plastic bag using a rolling pin.

1. First, make the Caramelized Pineapple. This can be made a week in advance and stored in the refrigerator in an airtight container.
2. Line two 12-cup muffin pans with cupcake liners and spoon a couple of teaspoons of the pineapple in the bottom of each one. Set them aside while you make the Vanilla Cupcake batter.
3. Fill the cupcake liners (with caramelized pineapple in place) three-quarters full of batter, and bake until the tops of the cupcakes are firm and a cake tester inserted in the center of a middle cupcake comes out with just a few crumbs, about 20 minutes. Let the cupcakes cool for 5 minutes in the pans before removing to a rack to cool completely.
4. While the cupcakes cool, make the Coconut Rum Buttercream.
5. Place the buttercream in a pastry bag fitted with a large star tip (Ateco #828). Pipe a generous swirl on top of each cupcake.
6. Sprinkle the cupcake with toasted coconut and top with a maraschino cherry and a paper umbrella.
7. Serve on a bed of graham cracker "sand."

DESTINATION: SEATTLE

I couldn't leave out my beloved city, so here are some ideas for yet another destination party—great for a homesick Seattleite away from the Emerald City or a grad about to depart.

SET THE STAGE

- Use classic imagery from this great city: the Space Needle, Pike Place Market, majestic pine trees, and the ferries that glide across Puget Sound. Incorporate plaid in honor of the great outdoors and Seattle's grunge era. Think outdoorsy urban, combining gray with natural wood and forest green. Display abundant amounts of fresh-cut flowers (dahlias are Seattle's official flower) in silver galvanized buckets, reminiscent of our famous Pike Place Market.

GET CRAFTY

- For a classic look, make Pennant Garlands (see page 53) made from scanned images of the Seattle Flag or an iconic Seattle image. Or get real and think rainy-day decor (yes, out-of-towners, it rains constantly!) with umbrellas or gray paper pom-poms (see How to Make Tissue Paper Pom-Poms, page 146) hanging from the ceiling. Inside each umbrella or paper "cloud" attach fishing lines and adhere metallic paper "raindrops." For a coffee-focused affair, make coffee filter garlands by flattening them and stringing them onto heavy thread or twine with a long needle. Filters can be dyed to match your color palette.

SEATTLE IN 24 HOURS: MY TOP 5 PICKS

My hometown offers much more than its famous gray skies, mountain vistas, and coffeehouses—all of which I dearly love. Here are some of my favorite local places and things to do when you only have 24 hours in Seattle. Come visit us!

- Buy vintage trinkets at Watson Kennedy, unique collectibles at Susan Wheeler Home, and/or handmade cards and delicate jewelry at Curtis Steiner.
- Eat Washington oysters at The Walrus and the Carpenter.
- Wander Melrose Market (I especially love lunch at Sitka & Spruce and small bouquets at Marigold and Mint)
- Ride a ferry to Bainbridge Island.
- Take a late-afternoon stroll through Olympic Sculpture Park and watch the sunset from the Seattle Great Wheel, Seattle's waterfront Ferris wheel.

ENTERTAIN THEM

- Host a coffee "cupping" (tasting) with some of Seattle's best roasts. Make mixed CDs of famous Seattle tunes as favors (and to play during your party). Send guests home with goody bags filled with Seattle's best artisan treats (Theo chocolate bars, Fran's Chocolates gray salt caramels, Top Pot Doughnuts, and your favorite Seattle coffee beans).

SERVE UP BITES & SIPS

- Serve smoked salmon, oysters on the half shell, coffee rubbed–beef skewers (or try Seattle's celeb chef Tom Douglas' "Rub with Love"), Tim's Cascade Potato Chips, fish-and-chips, Rainier cherries in the summer, and locally produced cheeses (I love Beecher's Handmade Cheese). Don't forget Seattle's beer scene: set up a microbrew tasting bar. Fill ice tubs with Seattle's own DRY Soda.

GIVE THEM CUPCAKES

Espresso Bean Cupcakes

Seattle brought the coffeehouse craze to the United States from Europe, so why not serve espresso-infused cupcakes? Naturally, you'll want to go ultra local and use espresso beans from one of Seattle's famous coffee roasters, such as Caffé Vita, Lighthouse Roasters, or Starbucks (all these beans are available online).

MAKES 2 DOZEN CUPCAKES

What You Need:

- **Chocolate Cupcakes**, recipe on page 188
- **Espresso Buttercream**, recipe on page 203
- Coffee sprinkles
- Chocolate-covered espresso beans (optional)

1. Make the Chocolate Cupcakes.
2. While the cupcakes cool, make the Espresso Buttercream.
3. Place the buttercream in a pastry bag fitted with a star tip (Ateco #828) and pipe a high swirl on each cupcake. Top with coffee sprinkles. A chocolate-covered espresso bean is a nice touch too!

COLORFUL CHARACTERS

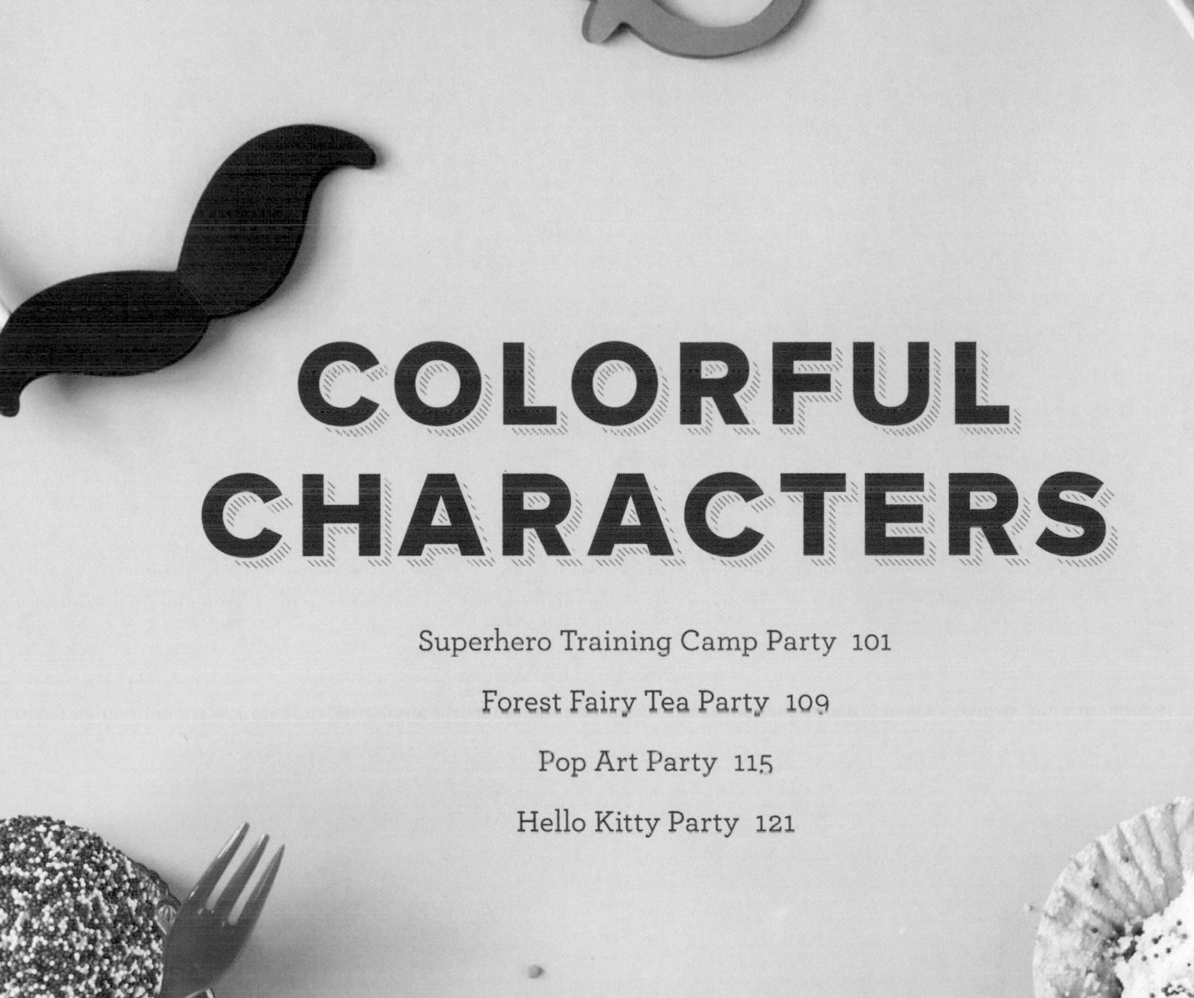

Remember when you were young and the world of make-believe seemed right within reach? When—if you just wished hard enough—you could actually travel into the pages of fairy tales, comic books, and movies to go on magical adventures?

For many children, their favorite stories' characters and places are vividly real . . . in their imaginations. A party themed around these made-up characters—whether fiction or a dreamt-up person or idea—can help bring that fantasy to life, if just for one day.

Even grown-ups can have fun with this theme, developing a party around a favorite artist, historical person, character from a novel or film, or childhood memory. And whether your party is based on an imaginary unicorn or Captain Kidd, your guests will be smitten by the creative spirit.

SUPERHERO TRAINING CAMP PARTY

Sure, you can create an incredible kids' party around an existing superhero like Superman or Wonder Woman. But granting superpowers to the guest of honor is a truly special gift and invites the child to play within the powerful world of imagination.

By the time my son Fleetwood was two and a half, he began insisting that we call him by his superhero name: Blade. We're not sure where the name came from, but "Blade" declared his superpowers to be "growing flowers, walking across the street by myself, and chewing gum."

His Aunt Megan made him a cape adorned with his initials that he liked to pair with underwear atop track pants, a homemade mask, and whatever other bells and whistles he deemed "super" on any given day. Soon his powers grew to include "finding rainbows," "turning bad guys into good guys," and run-of-the-mill "flying." (We meddling parents, of course, had to suggest additional powers like "superkindness" and "making new friends" so that he'd grow up knowing those are also superpowers worth having!)

By the time Fleetwood's fourth birthday rolled around, I knew he would want a superhero theme for his party and was determined to pull out all the stops. So I got to work creating a Superhero Training Camp, where he and his friends could spend the day as superheroes.

Kids are naturally imaginative, so it's easy to help them channel their own inner superhero. The Superhero Training Camp Questionnaire (visit the Printables section of TrophyCupcakes.com/book) is a fun exercise for kids *and* parents—though younger kids might need help with answers. Include it along with the party invitation so guests are ready for Training Camp when they arrive. When you and your own superkid fill it out, use the answers to help inspire decor, games, food, and other party elements.

The Superhero Party is fun for lots of kids' celebrations, especially Halloween, back-to-school, and National Superhero Day (April 28).

SET THE STAGE

Go for Color

- Pair your child's favorite color with a metallic tone that evokes indestructible force fields, metal batarangs (bat-shaped boomerangs), and golden lassos. To create a color palette, pair a couple of comic book–style oversaturated colors, such as royal blue, crimson red, canary yellow, or lime green, and accent them with black or a metallic tone. For Fleetwood's party, I went with his favorite colors of the moment: neon pink and lime green, with silver and black accents.

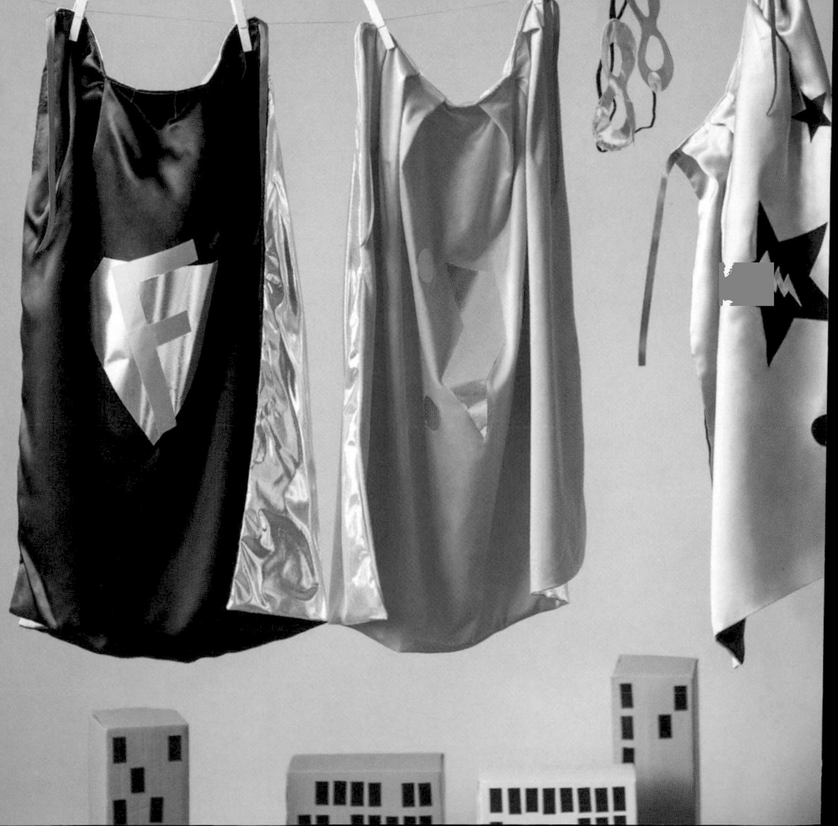

Decorate

- Superheroes need a logo, so the first order of business is to make a monogram. Sounds hard, right? Nope, even a mere mortal (with a few computer skills) can do it. Just pick a fun font, such as "Superhero" or "Badaboom BB" (both free at DaFont.com), and print out your superkid's first initial. Then copy and paste that over a shape, such as a diamond (à la Superman's logo), lightning bolt, or starburst.
- The logo will be a key decor element, going on invitations, favor bags, cupcakes, and more. I used a classic diamond shape for my son Fleetwood's party—he liked that diamonds are the hardest known naturally occurring material. But you should employ your kid's favorite motif, whether it's a rainbow, unicorn, star, or lightning bolt.
- Once you have a logo and a color palette, blanket the party in them. For this party, I used pink and lime green paper plates and napkins atop tables covered in black tablecloths adorned with silver and black cutouts of our diamond motif (simply paint the motif on cardboard and cut out when dry.) I also hung more diamond cutouts around the party space along with silver balloons and a clothesline complete with "superhero kits" full of ready-to-be decorated capes, masks, and cuffs (see Get Crafty, below).
- For the cupcake table I made a hero-worthy cityscape out of cardboard boxes to use as risers. Paint different-sized rectangular boxes gray with smaller black squares for "windows" (or use pieces of electrical tape to create windows) so they look like skyscrapers.

PRO-TIP

Paper plates are perfect (and perfectly acceptable) for kids' parties, picnics, casual affairs, and the like.

GET CRAFTY

Superhero Creation Station

- A Superhero Creation Station is a big highlight of this party. For each child, you'll need a plain cape, along with a mask, and a set of wristbands (if you like). Make capes and accessories using a pattern from your local fabric store (I adapted the ones for this party from McCalls pattern #6626), or purchase them online at SewPlainJane.com or from one of the many geniuses at Etsy.com.
- Before guests arrive, set up a table loaded with fabric stickers you've made ahead of time in an array of colors and shapes, including a sticker of each kid's initial. Set up the table near the individual "superhero kits": undecorated mask, cape, and wristbands. Watch everyone's eyes light up when they see these!
- Make the fabric stickers using mounting adhesive sheets, double-sided sticky paper that turns *anything* into a sticker. Simply peel off the backing, lay fabric cut to the

same size as the paper on top, and cut out the initials and motifs of your choice. When you peel the paper off the other side—*Shazam!*—a superhero sticker!

- Encourage your young guests to personalize their costumes for an hour while you get ready for the world's greatest gathering of superfriends! (Note: Puff paint, fake jewels, and glue would be fun, but they won't dry in time for the kids to wear their costumes during the party.)

♫ ENTERTAIN THEM

- Nothing gets superheroes revved up for action like inspiring theme music. Create a playlist of classic superhero themes, such as the ones from the Mighty Mouse, Batman, Superman, and Wonder Woman TV shows and movies, then watch your group take flight (or at least pretend to).

Superhero Obstacle Course

- To make the Training Camp Party complete, create a fun Superhero Obstacle Course. Depending on space considerations (and the age of your trainees), you can make a simple course with two or three obstacle stations, or a more advanced course with five or more stations.

- Create small stickers (visit the Printables section of TrophyCupcakes.com/book) for each station so trainees can add stickers to their capes as they complete the obstacles. Right before singing "Happy Birthday," present each trainee with an official "Certificate of Completion" (visit the Printables section of TrophyCupcakes.com/book).

- Use these ideas to customize a course for your own superkid:

  Superstrength Station—Have your superheroes lift and leap over some of the buildings from your hero-worthy cityscape (see Set the Stage: Decorate, page 103). This also makes a great photo op!

  X-Ray Vision Station—Test vision skills with a *Where's Waldo?*–style search-and-find puzzler appropriate for your guests' age group.

  Sensational Speed Station—Create a short sprinting course with cone obstacles.

  Fantastic Flight Station—Have guests demonstrate jumping skills with their five highest jumps. You could also rent a small trampoline or bouncy house.

  Enduring Balance Station—Create a low balance beam with a sturdy, brightly painted two-by-four secured to cinder blocks (or have two adults hold the beam in place). For younger kids, place the "beam" directly on the ground. Tape thick foam or pillows around the blocks to cushion any falls.

F
F
F
F
F
F
F
F

SERVE UP BITES & SIPS

- Feed your supergroup invigorating foods to enhance their powers: "hero" PB&Js cut into diamond, star, or lightning-bolt shapes; granola "power" bars; super-vision sticks (carrots); speed orbs (frozen grapes); kryptonite antidote (savory corn puffs); and thirst-quenching "power punch" and "energy-ade."
- For Fleetwood's party, I packaged and labeled the snacks individually, then neatly packed them into silver lunch boxes. I labeled the lunch boxes "Power Packs" and made a sign saying they were "For Superhero Trainees Only." You could also use gable boxes in the color of your choice (made of sturdy folded paper and available online) for the Power Packs as well.

GIVE THEM CUPCAKES

Planet Pop Rocks Cupcakes

Pop Rocks candies and cupcakes are an unbeatable combination. The saturated colors of the "rocks" look like minerals from a faraway planet, and kids go crazy for the sizzling, crackling effect.

MAKES 2 DOZEN CUPCAKES

What You Need:

Cupcakes in your child's favorite flavor: **Chocolate Cupcakes** (recipe on page 188) or **Vanilla Cupcakes** (recipe on page 182) are generally best for kids' parties

Vanilla Buttercream, recipe on page 198, perhaps tinted in your kid's superhero color

Pop Rocks (in one or more superhero colors) or edible glitter (see Toppings Glossary, page 31)

Superhero Cupcake Pick (optional)

1. Make the cupcakes.
2. While the cupcakes cool, make the Vanilla Buttercream.
3. Hand-frost the cupcakes in a dome shape (see Trophy Frosting Techniques, page 32).
4. Sprinkle Pop Rocks (or edible glitter) on top of each cupcake to create your planets.
5. If desired, add a superhero monogram cupcake pick to each cupcake. Cut a diamond shape out of silver glitter paper and a letter of your choice out of black paper. Glue the letter onto the diamond, then the diamond onto a toothpick. KaBlam! Superhero cupcake pick!

FOREST FAIRY TEA PARTY

Imaginative children know that mystical creatures live deep in lush, mossy forests in faraway lands. These magical sprites are incredibly rare and bring good luck to all who see them.

Naturally, a fairy-themed tea party will bring these magnificent woodland creatures to life and create a spirited afternoon for imaginative little kids with a taste for the fantastic. You can go all-out classic sparkly fairy or choose more of an eco-theme, focusing on natural woodland elements, as I did. This party is marvelous for sleepovers and birthdays . . . but could also work for an adult party, like a baby shower or a Mother's Day tea, with a few changes.

SET THE STAGE

Go for Color

- Entice all friends of the forest with a soothing palette of natural wood, mossy mint green, and forest floor colors of lavender, yellow, and pink. If you prefer to go more classic, choose forest green, toadstool red, and magenta or deep purple—or whatever color is the guest of honor's favorite.

Decorate

- This party is centered on the magic of the forest as well as tea, so the centerpiece should be a fantastical, foresty tea table. Lots of "mossy" decorations can be found online, including lush table runners to cover the length of a long, rectangular table. Atop the table runner, nestle tiny vases filled with small flowers, birds' nests with candy eggs, smooth rocks (you could also paint them in your color scheme), faux toadstools, and a variety of candlesticks and votive holders (for younger children use flameless candles. I covered glass votives in faux *bois* (fake wood pattern) sticky shelf liner.
- Move a dining table outside for an unexpected twist, perhaps under a tree or in a forested area. Anchor each chair with a set of fairy or butterfly wings. I particularly love hand dyed Waldorf-style silk wings; find them on Etsy.com from ZiezoDesigns.
- A tea party is an exciting treat, so set the table as you would for a fancy high tea, with an eco-twist if you like: I used bamboo plates, pretty glasses, and wooden tiered cake stands. For a more classic feel, break out the pretty china, glass stemware, and all the accoutrements. This is a great opportunity to finally use Grandma's silver tea set

and floral teapots! You can also find a mix of vintage china pieces in thrift stores for a colorful, madcap display.

- For adults, tweak this party into a Forest Tea Party. Forego the wings and wands, if you like, and simply whip up a magical spread. For a baby shower, you could still have guests make a wand and attach a wish for the mother or baby. Simply provide colorful paper, pens, and a hole punch, and have each guest write their wish and attach to the wand along with the feathers (see Get Crafty, below). This would be equally special for Mother's Day, a bridal shower, or a graduation party.

GET CRAFTY

God's Eye Fairy Wand

Along with fairy wings, each guest absolutely, positively *must* have a magic wand. And your guests will love their wands all the more when they make them themselves. For this party, I chose rustic wands, inspired by a classic camp craft, using real twigs plus yarn in my color scheme, but feel free to make a more glittery variety if that's what your fairy wants.

SUPPLIES

- 18-inch and 4-inch twigs for each wand (about the same thickness as a pencil)
- 1 skein of yarn total for each guest, in various colors: mossy mint green, lavender, yellow, pink, or whatever colors are in your palette
- Scissors
- Colorful feathers and/or pony beads

1. Start by making a cross with the two twigs: the small twig should be about 4 inches from the top of the long one. Wrap the point where the twigs meet diagonally a few times with yarn (making an X) to secure the twigs together.

2. Begin looping the yarn around each twig going all the way over, then under, and then clockwise to the next twig, repeating as necessary. If you'd like to switch yarn colors at any point, simply cut the yarn you're using and tie it onto the new color with a knot (trim ends and hide the knot in the back of your "eye").

3. Continue wrapping until you're done with your eye, then wrap the wand handle with yarn, switching colors about every inch or two.

4. Decorate your wand with feathers and/or beads attached to the corners of the eye with more yarn.

PRO-TIP

Straight willow branches make good fairy wands and are available at some nurseries and home improvement shops.

ENTERTAIN THEM

- The fairies will be endlessly entertained with crafting their magic wands, having tea and cakes, and flying around the magical forest you've created for them. Send each forest fairy home with their wings and wand, along with a little drawstring burlap or jute pouch with painted rocks, a meringue mushroom (recipes available online) in a little glassine bag, and a larger, glitter-filled glassine bag. Have your child write "Fairy dust—thank you for making my party magical!" on the bag, and fill it with different types of glitter and confetti, such as superfine, butterflies, and dots. Sew the top of each bag shut with thread, or seal with a sticker. Be sure to coordinate the glitter, thread, and sticker to the party's color palette. For adult parties, place sachets of fragrant tea and a few tea cookies in each bag along with a heartfelt thank-you note.

SERVE UP BITES & SIPS

- One of the nicest perks of serving classic high tea is that the foods are really quite simple: sandwiches, scones, and sweets. Tiny tea sandwiches are inexpensive, easy to make, and can be prepared ahead of time. Serve kid-friendly sandwiches of butter and jam or peanut butter and jelly. Make the sandwiches with classic white sandwich bread, slice off the crusts, and cut them into dainty triangles. If you like, use cookie cutters to create cute butterflies and other magical shapes. For adults, serve traditional and tasty combinations like cucumber and butter, smoked salmon and dill cream cheese and egg salad with watercress.
- For dessert, serve a variety of tea cookies, scones, crumpets, miniature fruit skewers, and, of course, Hummingbird Cupcakes (see page 112)—perfect for forest fairies. Serve herbal tea in beautiful pots along with colorful rock candy stir sticks. For younger children who may not be ready for hot tea, serve juice or milk from teapots.

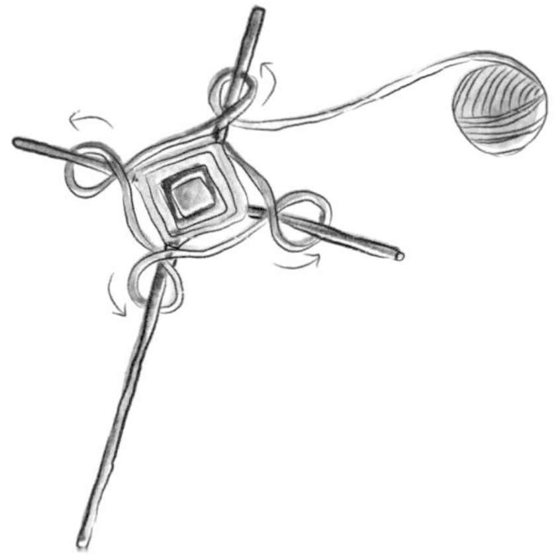

GIVE THEM CUPCAKES

Hummingbird Cupcakes

Hummingbird cake is a traditional Southern cake filled with ripe bananas, coconut, and pineapple. Some say it earned this name because the sweet cake would attract hummingbirds if you left it on a windowsill to cool. And some say it's because you can't help but make a yummy *hummmmming* sound when you eat it. I'll let you be the judge.

MAKES 2 DOZEN CUPCAKES

What You Need:

Hummingbird Cupcakes, recipe on page 190

Cream Cheese Buttercream, recipe on page 200

Blue and pink sanding sugar (optional)

Edible glitter sprinkles (optional)

1. Make the Hummingbird Cupcakes.
2. While the cupcakes cool, make the Cream Cheese Buttercream.
3. Place the buttercream in a pastry bag fitted with a large round tip (Ateco #809) to pipe a low swirl on each cupcake.
4. Sprinkle with the sanding sugar like we do at Trophy or with more "fairy appropriate" edible glitter for this particular party.

PRO-TIP

Miniature versions of the God's Eye Fairy Wands make stunning cupcake picks. Just start with shorter, thinner sticks (5 inches and 3 inches), and follow the instructions in Get Crafty, page 110.

Set the Stage — Pop Art Colors
Get Crafty — Banana Fringe Garland
Entertain Them — Polaroid Photobooth
Serve Up Bites + Sips — Andy's Candy Cocktails
Give them Cupcakes — Bananas Foster Cupcakes

POP ART PARTY

Make-believe parties aren't just for children. Grown-ups like to let their imaginations run wild too! Dreaming about the ultimate party fantasyland, I pondered: Who is history's consummate party host or hostess? Who threw the most over-the-top affairs that dazzled, perplexed, and delighted, all at the same time?

Naturally, I decided it was Andy Warhol, the most fabulous party animal ever. Not only was his legendary New York Factory a haven for the era's glitterati, but Warhol also knew how to mix an eclectic crowd, once quipping, "I always say, one's company, two's a crowd, and three's a party." So this one's for you, Andy!

The Pop Art Party is a blast for Halloween, art gallery and club openings, and New Year's Eve—frankly, pretty much any kind of adult party.

SET THE STAGE

Go for Color

- There are endless options to make your Pop Art Party pop—just extract the palette from a favorite Warhol artwork! Andy created electrifying silkscreen portraits of icons such as Marilyn Monroe and Michael Jackson in just two or three vibrant tones. Consider teal, yellow, and pink with a silver accent; red, royal blue, and emerald; or tangerine, pink, and aqua. Choose your favorite portrait and go with it.

Decorate

- Create an invitation featuring the guest of honor's portrait "Warholized" in his iconic digital silkscreen style. How do you do that? Luckily, The Andy Warhol Museum has developed The Warhol: DIY POP, an app for your iPhone, iPad, and iPod Touch that does the hard work for you. Forget about dragging out the paint cans; this app splashes color across any photograph, as if Warhol himself were behind the roller. You can even customize colors to match your vision. For the invite, simply print out your Warholized image in whatever size you like and either write the party details on the back or glue to an invitation with a blank front and printed details inside.

- Make sure your invite encourages guests to come dressed in the spirit of the party, as Andy himself or members of his Factory gang. He loved talking about parties almost as much as throwing them, so incorporate his own words, such as "The idea of waiting for something makes it more exciting," or "I have Social Disease. I have to go out every night."

- To re-create the feel of Warhol's Factory, arrange small couches (Andy's infamous couch was red), ottomans, pillows, and chaise lounges into intimate seating areas.

The real Factory was covered in aluminum foil, silver spray paint, silver balloons, and even silver glitter. So use aluminum foil as a runner on your buffet—or everywhere! Add silver balloons drifting around the space and silver glitter and paint wherever you can. Andy loved magazines and juicy gossip, so have the latest copies of *Interview* (the magazine he founded), as well as celebrity gossip rags like *National Inquirer*, laying around. Stack Campbell's soup cans and Brillo boxes on open surfaces as pop art.

- Andy wore tortoiseshell and clear plastic sunglasses in the Ray-Ban Wayfarer shape. Find cheap knockoffs, remove the "glass," and spray-paint the frames in your party palette. Present guests with a pair as they enter so they can get in the Factory spirit.

GET CRAFTY

Banana Fringe Garlands

The silkscreen banana graphic created by Warhol for The Velvet Underground's first album is a fun and iconic image of the era, so make it a centerpiece of your party. In fact, why not make bananarrific garlands?

SUPPLIES (PER GARLAND):

- 15 sheets of 20-by-30-inch tissue paper
- Sewing machine or stapler
- 15 feet of 2-inch ribbon
- Scissors
- Rotary cutter and self-healing mat (optional)
- 25 pieces of sturdy card stock
- Craft glue

1. Layer 3 sheets of tissue and fold in half lengthwise.
2. Sew the top edge of tissue about ½ inch from the folded edge. (Or staple every 3 inches, if you prefer.) Repeat with the rest of the tissue. You will have five 10-by-30-inch pieces.
3. Fold the ribbon lengthwise over the top fold of the tissue, leaving 18 inches at either end. Glue or sew in place. Overlap lengths of tissue slightly as you go. You should now have all five pieces attached to your ribbon.
4. Using scissors or a rotary cutter on a self-healing mat, cut 1-inch strands (vertically) down the entire length of the garland. Be sure not to cut into the ribbon along the top.
5. Download a picture of the banana from the Internet and print 25 color copies on sturdy card stock. (Make the bananas about 8 to 12 inches tall for the best impact.)
6. Cut out the banana shapes and glue the tops of the bananas to the garland.
7. Repeat to make as many garlands as possible, and hang them everywhere, especially around central party features such as the food or dessert table, or the cocktail bar.

ENTERTAIN THEM

- This one is easy: you *must* have a dance party. Wait until the party is in full swing—but not too late—to clear the floor and turn up the music. Be sure to make a playlist of musicians hip to the scene in the '60s, '70s, and early '80s—especially The Velvet Underground, Duran Duran, and David Bowie, who all wrote songs about Andy. Mick Jagger and Bob Dylan also frequented the Factory and were part of Andy's in-crowd.

- I always advocate photo stations, and since Andy was a Polaroid junkie, photographs are a must for this party. Make a photo backdrop by hanging lots of loose strips of aluminum foil and thin silver streamers from ceiling to floor or more of your fringe garland (see Get Crafty, page 116). Assemble a dress-up box of life-size masks taken from Andy's portraits, such as Marilyn Monroe, Mao Tse-tung, Elizabeth Taylor, Jackie Kennedy, and Michael Jackson. (To create the masks, make life-size color prints of the celebrities' heads, mount them on stiff card stock, cut out the shape of the head and holes for the eyes with a utility knife, and adhere a small stick to one side of the head—like a masquerade ball mask.)

- Add a few Warhol-style wigs and other glittery, colorful, crazy ones, plus props like empty champagne bottles, Super 8 cameras, and candy cigarettes. Rather than taking digital photos, play like Andy and take Polaroids! The cameras and film are experiencing a comeback: both the film and new and vintage models can be found on eBay. There's no need to have a designated cameraman; encourage guests to take Polaroids of each other. (If you live in Seattle, Rare Medium, a Polaroid boutique and repair shop in the Capitol Hill neighborhood, sells refurbished cameras and new film; RareMediumSeattle.com.) Polaroid.com also offers lots of great modern instant cameras.

"OH, I ONLY EAT CANDY."

How could we not be absolutely fascinated by Andy Warhol? In their book, *What the Great Ate*, authors Matthew and Mark Jacob report that "Andy Warhol would visit pastry shops daily, sometimes bringing home an entire birthday cake and eating it by himself. At sumptuous meals, he would abstain, explaining, 'Oh, I only eat candy.' One time at an airport, his bag was searched at customs and was found to be full of candy, chewing gum, and cookies. After his death, his collection of cookie jars was auctioned off for a quarter of a million dollars."

SERVE UP BITES & SIPS

Naturally, you should serve Campbell's tomato soup, with additional cans used as decor on the table, alongside bite-size grilled cheese sandwiches. Andy was a fan of ready-made 1950s-style meals, and individual TV dinners paired with glasses of champagne—his favorite drink. Since Andy adored candy, for a signature drink, I created a candy cocktail.

Andy's Candy Cocktail

Rainbow nonpareils, to rim glass (see Toppings Glossary, page 31)

1 ounce vodka

1 ounce lemon juice

½ ounce triple sec

½ ounce banana liqueur

Champagne float

Lollipop, for a swizzle stick

Rim a martini glass with nonpareils. Combine the vodka, lemon juice, triple sec, and banana liqueur in a shaker about half full of ice. Shake well and strain into the glass. Top with champagne and drop in the lollipop. (I love handmade lollies from This Charming Candy in Seattle.) For even more swizzle fun, glue a metallic silver pom-pom on the end of each lolly!

HOW TO RIM A GLASS: To rim a glass in sprinkles or edible glitter, fill a shallow flat saucer or container with about ⅛ inch of Simple Syrup (recipe on page 85) and another saucer with ½ inch of your sprinkle of choice. Be sure the saucers are large enough to dip the rim of your glass in. Dip the rim of the glass in the simple syrup then into the sprinkles or glitter (or salt, for margaritas).

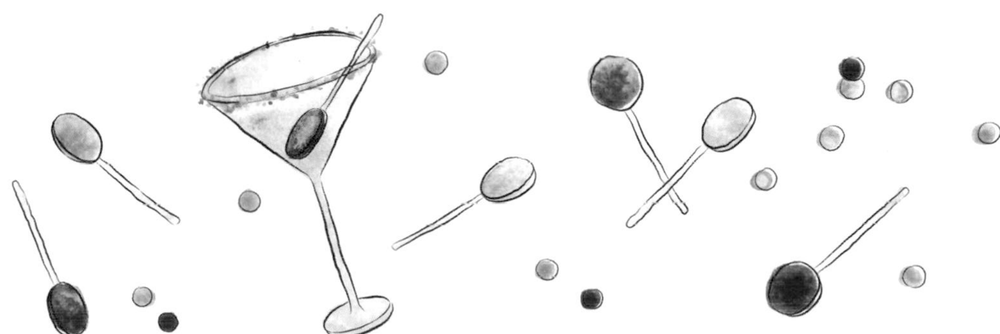

GIVE THEM CUPCAKES

Bananas Foster Cupcakes

One good banana deserves another, so continue the Warhol-style banana theme with Trophy's Bananas Foster Cupcakes. From the decadent caramel sauce to the fancy flame finale—which can be a little tricky—we've turned this exotic dessert into a dreamy, delicious cupcake. It all starts with rich banana cake and a caramelicious filling. Then it's topped with a mountain of toasted rum meringue and a crisp banana chip. It's pure Bananas Foster flavor in a handy cupcake form.

MAKES 2 DOZEN CUPCAKES

What You Need:

Brown Sugar Caramel, recipe on page 215

Banana Cupcakes, recipe on page 191

Rum Meringue Frosting, recipe on page 199

Nonpareils in pop art colors (optional)

24 banana chips (optional)

Apple corer

Kitchen torch

PRO-TIP

Add a pop with mini paper banana cupcake picks. Print out 1½-inch versions of the banana used on page 116, cut them out, hot glue them to food picks, and place one in each cupcake.

1. Make the Brown Sugar Caramel and set aside to cool. (It can be made up to a week in advance and stored in the refrigerator in an airtight container. Bring to room temperature before using.)
2. Make the Banana Cupcakes.
3. When the cupcakes are cool, fill each with a generous amount of Brown Sugar Caramel (see How to Fill a Cupcake, page 179).
4. Make the Rum Meringue Frosting.
5. Place the frosting in a pastry bag fitted with a large star tip (Ateco #867) and pipe a triple swirl of meringue on each cupcake.
6. For Andy-style, sprinkle cupcakes with the nonpareils and top with banana cupcake picks (see Pro-Tip, left).

Make Them Trophy

For Trophy-style cupcakes, use a kitchen torch to brown the meringue by lightly brushing the flame close to the meringue until it's brown (be careful not to get too close and burn or catch the meringue or the cupcake liners on fire.

Top each cupcake with a banana chip. Serve immediately or within 2 hours.

HELLO KITTY PARTY

I just can't get enough of colorful character party themes and I just couldn't leave Hello Kitty out of the fun . . . so here's a few more party-puuurfect ideas!

SET THE STAGE

- The Hello Kitty guest of honor is bright and kind-hearted, and loves to collect all things cute. This party is particularly easy to create because adorable Hello Kitty party supplies are available in copious amounts at Sanrio stores, party shops, and online, including at TrophyCupcakes.com. Start by sending a cute Hello Kitty invitation with all of the party details. For a Miss Kitty White–approved bash, simply decorate with Hello Kitty table coverings, garlands, trinkets, plates and napkins, endless pink and white pom-poms (see How to Make Tissue Paper Pom-Poms, page 146), plus plenty of bows and balloons.

GET CRAFTY

- Let the guests do the crafting for this party. Set up a birthday-hat decorating station so everyone can make a custom cone chapeau with Hello Kitty in mind. Provide a plain pink birthday hat for each guest. Plain cone hats are available at party supply shops or you can make your own (visit the Printables section of TrophyCupcakes.com/book). Supply craft glue, lots of Hello Kitty stickers, pink and white pom-poms, pink and red rickrack, and red bows—Miss Kitty's trademark!

ENTERTAIN THEM

- Attach red (or pink) bows to the guests' hair. Give them friendship books, plus stickers and plastic jewels to decorate them with. They can then sign each other's books with fun, secret messages. For favors, endless Hello Kitty trinkets—including my personal favorite, Hello Kitty PEZ dispensers—can easily be found online. Friendship bracelets also make great favors with pink and white embroidery floss, of course. Either make them ahead of time or have guests make them at the party for a make-and-take favor. (Instructions for how to macramé friendship bracelets are easily found online.)

SERVE UP BITES & SIPS

- Serve bow-tie (or Hello Kitty–shaped!) pasta; tea sandwiches with pink cream cheese cut into heart, flower, or Hello Kitty shapes; pink lemonade; and pink sodas with pink-and-white-striped straws and little red bows—anything you can make over-the-top cute or anything pink.

Strawberry Cheesecake Cupcakes

Don't let this pretty little cupcake fool you—Trophy's Strawberry Cheesecake Cupcake is downright decadent. It is moist strawberry cake filled with rich strawberry preserves, on top of a graham cracker crust, finished off with strawberry cream cheese buttercream and a luscious strawberry fresh from the farmers' market.

MAKES 2 DOZEN CUPCAKES

What You Need:

- **Graham Cracker Crust**, recipe on page 216
- **Strawberry Cupcakes**, recipe on page 192
- **Strawberry Cream Cheese Buttercream**, recipe on page 204
- 1½ cups of strawberry preserves or jam
- 2 dozen strawberries or small candy flowers (optional)
- 1 cup crushed graham cracker mixed with ¼ cup sanding sugar (optional)
- Apple corer

PRO-TIP

To save time, make the crust up to a week in advance. Store in an airtight container.

1. Make the Graham Cracker Crust.
2. Make the Strawberry Cupcakes.
3. Fill the cupcake liners (with the graham cracker crusts in place) three-quarters full with the cupcake batter, and bake until the tops of the cupcakes are firm, and a cake tester inserted in the center of a middle cupcake comes out with just a few crumbs, about 20 minutes. The cupcakes should still be very pale and turn golden only around the edges. Let the cupcakes cool for 5 minutes in the pans before removing to a rack to cool completely.
4. While the cupcakes cool, make the Strawberry Cream Cheese Buttercream.
5. Fill each cooled cupcake with thick strawberry preserves or jam (see How to Fill a Cupcake, page 179).
6. For this party, use Ateco tip #828 to pipe a classic swirl, then sprinkle cupcakes with white nonpareils and pink sanding sugar. Top them with a cute Hello Kitty ring.

Make Them Trophy

Hand-frost each cupcake flat (see page 32) with an offset spatula, and edge with a mix of crushed graham cracker and sanding sugar (see How to Edge a Cupcake, page 31). Top with a small strawberry or candy flower.

TAKE
UT
ROLL
MAN
U.S.A.
SECTION Orch
ROW N
SEAT 12
AISLE E
PRICE 0.00
NEP
2006
STR.
Festival

FICTITIOUS FÊTES

Classic movies, beloved books, and favorite TV shows are nostalgic touchstones for so many of us, transporting us back to a carefree, romantic, or simply fun time in our lives. So why not create a party around a time-honored work of fiction?

Not only will your event be strikingly visual, it'll offer plenty of opportunities to "wink" at your guests through famous phrases or jokes. From classics (for example, *The Great Gatsby* and *Gone with the Wind*) to children's favorites (*The Berenstain Bears, Winnie-the-Pooh*) or pop-cultural mainstays (*The Dukes of Hazzard, Dallas*)—even contemporary shows like *Mad Men* and *Downton Abbey*—these familiar and adored story lines are themes your friends will appreciate and love participating in.

BERENSTAIN BEARS BIKE PARADE & PICNIC

"Get a bicycle. You will not regret it, if you live."
—**MARK TWAIN**, *Taming the Bicycle*

My family and I love riding bikes, as do many of our friends. In fact, a good friend of mine had a group bike ride for his birthday, and I thought, "We should do this more often!" After all, it's hard to beat a ride through the park on a warm summer day with people you love.

Then, thanks to the Berenstain Bears book *The Bike Lesson*, it hit me: why not host an annual bike parade and picnic for friends, family, and neighbors? The book was a childhood favorite of mine, and now my son loves it. In it, the father bear teaches his son to ride a bike through a series of clumsy "don't do that" lessons. This sweet story about learning as a family and spending time together was the perfect inspiration for a Bike Parade and Picnic party.

So gather your loved ones for a festive group bike-along, culminating in a delicious picnic feast—a fantastic annual tradition! This party is especially fun for family reunions and celebrating the last days of summertime and the Tour de France.

SET THE STAGE

Go for Color

- The unique combination of muted orange, butter yellow, denim blue, and navy recalls a bygone era of picnics and parades. Or take a cue straight from the Berenstain Bears and decorate in bright red, white, navy, and royal blue.

Decorate

- This is a two-part party—parade and picnic—so you'll want to create a fun invitation that gets people in the spirit and provides plenty of information. Create an invitation announcing the name of your party: for example, the "First Annual Williamson Family Bike Parade." Include such details as "Bring your bikes! We'll provide fun supplies for decorating them before a parade through the neighborhood. Afterwards, there will be a picnic, prizes, music, and fun for all." Print the details on 11-by-14-inch poster paper, roll it up, and tie with a pretty ribbon (or scan an image from *The Bike Lesson* onto card stock and write your party details by hand next to the image), and mail it in a small box with a pinwheel (see Get Crafty, page 129) or hand deliver them to friends and neighbors. I also love the e-invite "Let's Hit the Road Jack" on PaperlessPost.com.

- As for decorations, you'll want to embellish two separate environments: the staging/decorating area as well as the finish line/picnic area. A backyard or local park will make the perfect backdrop for your family picnic. Set up picnic tables or lots of colorful picnic blankets and big pillows so everyone can kick back and celebrate after the ride. Hang streamers, ribbons, and tissue paper balls or pom-poms (see How to Make Tissue Paper Pom-Poms, page 146) from trees. Make tricolor pinwheel lapel pins (see Get Crafty, below) for guests to wear for an old-time, Americana feeling.
- Add to the picnic spirit by packaging items in cute containers such as little glass jam jars, complete with colorful reusable or compostable party ware. Find wooden forks, knives, and spoons, and embellish them by dipping the ends of the handles in non-toxic paint to match your theme.

GET CRAFTY

Party-Perfect Pinwheels

To make any number of pinwheel crafts like cupcake picks, lapel pins, or barrettes, follow the same directions for Party-Perfect Pinwheels. For smaller pinwheels, just start with a smaller square.

SUPPLIES

- Two-sided colored paper or scanned or photocopied pages from *The Bike Lesson*
- Ruler
- Pencils
- Scissors
- Round-headed pins
- 12-inch dowels

1. Cut a 6-by-6-inch square out of the paper or photocopied pages. Place the paper face down.
2. On the back side, using your ruler, draw a line from the upper left corner to the bottom right corner, and from the top right to the bottom right, making an "X."
3. With scissors, cut each line from its corner point, stopping about 1 inch before the center of the "X."
4. Flip over the paper and neatly fold every other corner in toward the center, creating a pinwheel shape.
5. Secure a pin through the center of the pinwheel into a 12-inch dowel, and let it spin in the breeze!

ENTERTAIN THEM

- To get things off to a fun start, get your guests to trick out their bikes as if they were floats in a parade! Set out boxes of supplies and give them an hour or so to festoon their rides with crepe paper streamers, balloons, ribbons, flags, pinwheels, flowers, horns, tassels, bells, and playing cards (attach them to wheel spokes with clothespins to make festive noisemakers), as well as all kinds of wire, pipe cleaners, and tape to firmly adhere the decorations. After an hour, squeeze a bike horn and let the parade begin!

- Don't let the fun stop when the parade ends. After guests have replenished with a hearty picnic, host an awards ceremony and hand out ribbons for things like "Most Creative," "Most Colorful," and "Most Festive" bike decor. Make the awards yourself using cupcake liners (see Entertain Them, page 156).
- Stage a few fun races, such as tricycle relays (even more fun when grown-ups participate!), obstacle courses, and a one-leg pedal dash. Give top billing to any extra-talented kids in a bike performance talent show. Gather little ones on a blanket for a reading of *The Bike Lesson*. Fill activity baskets with Berenstain Bear coloring pages (available on PBS.org) or bicycle-themed coloring books and crayons to keep the kids busy all afternoon.

SERVE UP BITES & SIPS

- Individual picnic baskets are an adorable way to spoil your guests. Adhere colored ribbons to the front of each basket and fill them with sandwiches wrapped in white parchment paper tied with a ribbon, baked goods such as scones or muffins with individual jars of jam and butter, seasonal fruit, and artisanal crackers and slabs of cheese packaged in glassine or patterned treat bags. If individual picnic baskets feel like too much fuss, lay out a gourmet picnic buffet on a table festooned with a pretty checkered tablecloth.
- Serve ice-cold sodas in unexpected flavors. I love Seattle-based DRY Soda and its refreshing, not-too-sweet sodas in amazing flavors such as rhubarb and lavender. I also love serving natural Q Kola, bottled French lemonade, homemade sun tea, and, of course, plenty of cold water for everyone.

GIVE THEM CUPCAKES

Blueberry Pie Cupcakes

Nothing says summertime like fresh berries, especially when they're baked into a pie! So serve your hungry cyclists Blueberry Pie Cupcakes—gathering summer's yummiest elements into one delicious confection. We start with flaky pie crust on the bottom, then add house-made blueberry pie filling and mouthwatering Madagascar Bourbon vanilla cake. We top it all off with vanilla bean buttercream, a fresh blueberry, and a wee wedge of flaky pie crust. Set aside 4 hours to make what are Trophy's August "Flavor of the Month."

MAKES 2 DOZEN CUPCAKES

What You Need:

2 dozen Pie Crust Rounds and Garnishes, recipe on page 212

Blueberry Pie Filling, recipe on page 217

Vanilla Cupcakes, recipe on page 182

Vanilla Buttercream, recipe on page 198

2 teaspoons vanilla bean paste or the seeds from 1 scraped vanilla bean

2 dozen fresh blueberries

Sanding sugar

1. First, make the pie dough.

2. While the dough is chilling, make the Blueberry Pie Filling and set aside to cool.

3. Finish making the Pie Crust Rounds and Garnishes.

4. Line two 12-cup muffin pans with cupcake liners and place a cooled crust in the bottom of each one. Set the crusts aside while you make the Vanilla Cupcakes batter.

5. Fill the cupcake liners (with the pie crusts in place) three-quarters full and bake until the tops of the cupcakes are firm and a cake tester inserted in the center of a middle cupcake comes out with just a few crumbs, about 20 minutes. Let the cupcakes cool for 5 minutes in the pans before removing to a rack to cool completely.

6. While the cupcakes cool, make the Vanilla Buttercream, using the 2 teaspoons vanilla bean paste or the seeds from 1 scraped vanilla bean instead of the vanilla extract.

7. To assemble the cupcakes, start by generously filling the cupcake with blueberry pie filling (see How to Fill a Cupcake, page 179).

8. Place the buttercream in a pastry bag fitted with a large star tip (Ateco #828) and pipe a generous swirl of buttercream on each cupcake.

9. Top with a blueberry, a little sanding sugar, and one of the small pie crust garnishes.

PRO-TIP

To save time, make the pie crusts (and garnishes) and the blueberry pie filling at least a day in advance. See individual recipes for details.

CASABLANCA PARTY

You could plan an amazing party around pretty much any classic movie, once you start thinking about the creative possibilities. For a fiftieth wedding anniversary, I borrowed the motifs, visuals, and flavors from the amazing Bogart-Bergman film *Casablanca* to create an exotic, romantic, and sentimental gala affair.

The *Casablanca* theme is marvelous for anyone who loves the 1944 Academy Awards' Best Picture. But it's also for anyone who simply loves *love*—or Bogart and Bergman, or Morocco, or the thought of a party with a live pianist and champagne cocktails. Of course, this theme is especially apt for anniversary, engagement, and cocktail parties. I imagine it would be the perfect way to celebrate a couple who fell in love in Paris while watching this classic film—the inspiration for this magnificent fiftieth anniversary party.

SET THE STAGE

Go for Color

- Evoke the allure of old filmmaking with black-and-white decor accented with a deep red and saffron. Or use black and white as your base colors and add accents of plum and tangerine.

Decorate

- For a milestone anniversary, you'll want to really put the happy couple on a pedestal. So create the ultimate marquee invitation with a movie poster framing them in the classic Bogie and Bergman *Casablanca* cheek-to-cheek pose. Replace the poster's text with information about the party. You'll need to employ the help of a graphic artist or Photoshop-savvy friend, but the results will be fantastic! Once the image is designed, print it on invitation-sized card stock or, even better, as a full-size movie poster and mail them to invitees in poster tubes. Extra posters can be used to decorate the party space. For something a little simpler, the "Tangiers" e-invite on PaperlessPost.com is stunning.

- Transform your event space into Rick's Café Américain, circa World War II. Hire a pianist or find a venue with a piano—someone singing "As Time Goes By" is a must! Decorate with as many Moroccan lanterns as you can get your hands on. Create a film noir ambiance with lots of candlelight. Set the scene with café tables covered in white tablecloths, carved wood wall dividers, hanging ferns, potted palms, and simple floral arrangements of a single gardenia in water. For a milestone anniversary, you may also want to display photographs of the couple either in small frames on each table or grouped into a cluster on a larger table that guests can gather around for some reminiscing.

- Greet guests with something extra-special: paper wrist corsages for the women and mini boutonnieres for the men (see Get Crafty, below). Place them in a pretty basket at the door and tie them to ladies' wrists and pin them to men's lapels as they arrive.

GET CRAFTY

Tissue Paper Wrist Corsages and Mini Boutonnieres

Make paper wrist corsages and boutonnieres with small versions of Tissue Paper Pom-Poms (see How to Make Tissue Paper Pom-Poms, page 146).

SUPPLIES (MAKES 4)

- 5 sheets tissue paper (20-by-30-inch) in your party colors
- Scissors
- String
- 2 yards one-inch satin ribbon
- Pearl corsage pins, available at sewing and hobby stores

1. Layer all 5 sheets of tissue paper and fold (lengthwise) into a 1-inch accordion fold.
2. Cut the folded strip in 4 even pieces (you'll be able to make 4 flowers), secure the center of each piece with string, knot, and trim the ends.
3. For corsages, slide an 18-inch length of satin ribbon between the string and the tissue paper (this will make your wrist tie), then open the flower.
4. For boutonnieres, simply open the flowers and provide corsage pins.

ENTERTAIN THEM

- If you want to really wow your guests, hire a live piano player who can play and sing 1940s tunes and songs from the film, including "It Had to Be You." Set up the café tables around the piano, provide lyric sheets, and get everyone singing along. Create a poker den—a candlelit area with poker tables and a real dealer. Order personalized poker chips engraved with the name of the couple and the year they wed. Be sure to have a roulette wheel. Lucky number 22!

- I always recommend you hire a photographer for very special occasions such as milestone anniversaries. Often, occasions like these are the rare times that everyone in the family is all in one room. Capitalize on the reunion and be sure to get family portraits and group shots—and of course, plenty of photos with the happy couple.

- Send each guest home with a favor they'll cherish forever, such as a framed photo of the couple—vintage or modern, or even from that night. Many photographers are now able to set up equipment on-site that allows them to print photographs and have them ready for guests to take home as they leave. After the party, be sure to make an album as a special gift the guests of honor can cherish for many more years to come.

SERVE UP BITES & SIPS

- Set up a buffet of delicious Moroccan food. Consider *tagines* (slow-cooked stews of meats and vegetables) of spiced couscous and stewed chicken. Place big bowls of olives laced with orange peel on the table alongside pretty jars of preserved lemons and stacks of oranges studded with cloves. Serve chicken skewers with basmati rice—a nibble that adults and kids alike will love.
- For drinks, serve the good stuff: your favorite French bubbly and old-style champagne cocktails (see recipe, right) in vintage champagne coupes, just as in the movie. Create a signature cocktail (see How to Create Signature Cocktails, page 48) and call it Letter of Transit or We'll Always Have Paris. An elegant nonalcoholic punch served in a crystal punch bowl is also a lovely touch, especially when it's called Lisbon Punch (everyone in *Casablanca* was trying to get to Lisbon).

Champagne Cocktail

This is the classic recipe served by New York City's Metropolitan Hotel in the 1930s. Here's a fun factoid: The champagne cocktail was chosen by Esquire *magazine as one of the top ten cocktails of 1934.*

1 sugar cube
Angostura bitters
Chilled champagne or sparkling wine
Lemon twist, for garnish

- Soak a sugar cube with a couple of good splashes of Angostura bitters in the bottom of a large champagne flute. Fill slowly with champagne. Garnish with a lemon twist.

SHEA &
Please join us
NOVEMBER 27TH
6 PM
9393 OCEANSIDE BLVD.

GIVE THEM CUPCAKES

Casablanca Cupcakes

Get ready, this isn't like any Trophy cupcake you've tasted before! Flourless almond cakes are very popular in Morocco—as are orange- and rose-scented desserts. Orange almond cupcakes topped with rose-water buttercream—aka Casablanca Cupcakes—bring together the best of these exotic tastes. Bonus: This recipe is gluten-free.

MAKES 2 DOZEN CUPCAKES

What You Need:

Candied Rose Petals, recipe on page 217

Orange and Almond Cupcakes, recipe on page 193

Rose Water Buttercream, recipe on page 205

1. Two to three days before you need them, make the Candied Rose Petals.
2. Make the Orange and Almond Cupcakes.
3. While the cupcakes cool, make the Rose Water Buttercream.
4. Place the buttercream in a pastry bag fitted with a large round tip (Ateco #809) to pipe a small swirl on each cupcake. Garnish with a candied rose petal.

PRO-TIP

Serve the cupcakes on a large decorative platter covered with fragrant rose petals.

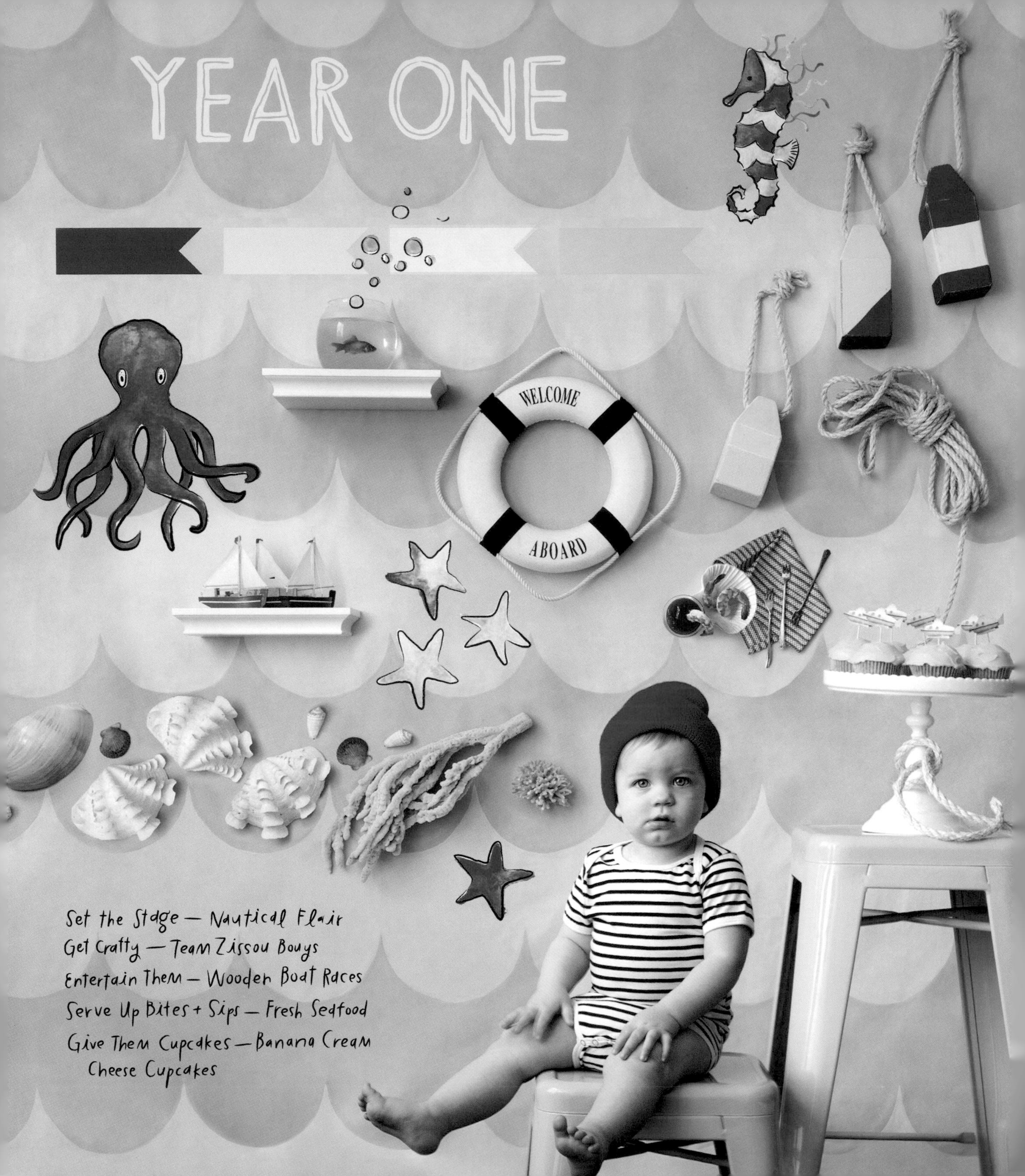
YEAR ONE
WELCOME
ABOARD
Set the Stage — Nautical Flair
Get Crafty — Team Zissou Bouys
Entertain Them — Wooden Boat Races
Serve Up Bites + Sips — Fresh Seafood
Give Them Cupcakes — Banana Cream Cheese Cupcakes

LIFE AQUATIC PARTY: BABY'S FIRST BIRTHDAY

I know what you're thinking: a first birthday party with a theme from Wes Anderson's film *The Life Aquatic with Steve Zissou*? To which I respond: *definitely!*

I love all things Wes Anderson, and his films' bright colors and fantastical imagery translate beautifully to party themes. I'm also a big believer in making a child's first birthday a "coming out" party of sorts for the parents. Think about it: the guest of honor is often the only baby in the room, and the occasion is usually the first opportunity all year for new parents to cut loose with friends and family. Some of the best parties I've been to were first birthdays! *The Life Aquatic* is a wonderful mix of childlike motifs and adult themes, so for me, it's the perfect first-year celebration. It's also great for beach and boating-season bashes—a fun spin on a traditional nautical-themed party.

SET THE STAGE

Go for Color

- A combination of red, aqua, and yellow perfectly captures childlike nautical imagery and *The Life Aquatic*'s distinct color palette.

Decorate

- Create magical imagery that you can use for the invitation as well as the party. Fashion a backdrop from an aqua-colored sheet painted with a scalloped wave motif in a slightly lighter or darker shade than your sheet. You could also hang aqua and green streamers, fringe, or festooning to create an aquatic background. Cover your backdrop in fishing nets, decorative fish, shells, buoys, nautical flags, or other sea-themed decor. Take a picture of your child dressed in nautical stripes or like Steve Zissou (in a red knit fisherman's cap and light blue shirt) in front of the backdrop and build the invitation around the imagery. Just about any nautical invitation will also do the trick.

- For decor, anything nautical goes! Miniature wooden boats, vintage buoys (see Get Crafty, page 140), fishing nets, large clamshells, nautical flags, fish decorations, and sand will conjure the smells and sounds of the ocean. At the very least, these props will help transport your guests to some faraway fishing village or the bow of Steve Zissou's ship!

GET CRAFTY

Team Zissou Buoys

After seeing photographs of the historic fishing village of Apalachicola, Florida (I'm dying to visit a shop called the Apalachicola Sponge Company and Smokehouse Antiques, by the way), I got so inspired by beautiful vintage buoys that I wanted to figure out a way to make my own. The salt-washed primary colors and simple striped patterns immediately bring to mind memories of my childhood fishing with my pop, and those rare, thrilling-to-a-child trips to see boats in the marina. I admit, you'll need a saw, a power drill, and some elbow grease for this craft . . . so if that's not your thing, you can also find authentic vintage buoys on eBay and reproductions on NauticalSeasons.com.

SUPPLIES

- 1 wooden four-by-four, cut down into 7-, 8-, and 9-inch sections (or the size you like); these are your buoys
- Hand saw
- Drill and ½-inch boring bit
- Paint in your party colors
- 1-inch-wide paint brush
- Coarse sand paper
- 1 yard of heavy ½-inch-diameter rope

1. Trim the "top" end of each buoy into a point with a hand saw (trim the top inch or so of the point off).
2. Drill a ½-inch hole near the top of each buoy.
3. Paint the buoys with large horizontal or diagonal stripes in your party colors. After the paint is dry, scuff up the finish with sandpaper to create a vintage look.
4. String a 1-foot length of rope through each hole, tie a knot in the ends, and go fish!

PRO-TIP

The hardware store can cut the four-by-fours down for you, usually for a small additional charge.

ENTERTAIN THEM

- Remember that backdrop you made for the invitation? It's going to make a marvelous setting for fun and wacky photos! Add a box of props like those seen in the movie, such as red knit caps, toy submarines and boats, a life ring, an acoustic guitar, and plastic lobsters, sea horses, and other ocean creatures. If you can find a plastic or lightweight porthole, that would be great fun for guests to peek through as well.
- Rent old Jacques Cousteau movies and marine-themed educational films (I especially love old 16mm cameras and reel-to-reel film spools) and screen them on a wall. Some libraries still loan or rent these out! You can also find vintage films on eBay.
- Ask a musically inclined friend (or hire an acoustic guitarist) to play songs from the movie. Or you could simply play the soundtrack mixed with like-minded songs.
- For children, set up a supervised wading pool or galvanized farm troughs in the backyard and stage balloon-powered wooden boat races (balloon-powered boats can be found in toy stores and online). Blow a whistle to start the race and they're off!

SERVE UP BITES & SIPS

- One-year-olds are not especially experimental eaters, so prepare your child's regular meal for the day, plus that extra-special "first cupcake." This party feast is for the grown-ups! Decorate a buffet table with nautical ropes and other props and pile it high with a gourmet seafood feast: giant clamshells (or shell-shaped platters) with oysters on the half shell, lobster rolls, chilled shrimp with cocktail sauce, and my superb Spicy Crab Toasts (see recipe, below). Don't forget the mini sub sandwiches wrapped in yellow paper, a tip of the hat to Team Zissou's magical yellow submarine.
- For the under-ten set, I often make a large pan of homemade macaroni and cheese for parties, so there will be a hearty dish on hand that everyone will love. You can find endless interesting variations online. I recommend the recipes on MarthaStewart.com.

Spicy Crab Toasts

Mix **1 cup freshly picked crabmeat** with **2 tablespoons mayonnaise**, **¼ teaspoon Sriracha hot sauce**, a **pinch of salt**, and a **squeeze of lemon**. Toast **thinly sliced bread**, cut it into bite-size pieces, and spoon a dollop of the crab mixture on top. Garnish with **cress**.

- For drinks, set up a casual table with cold beer (in galvanized buckets) and wine. For a fun kid-friendly drink, whip up a batch of Belafonte Punch—two parts lemonade to one part club soda—in a big glass spigot jar. Add a pint each of blueberries and strawberries for a festive nautical look and extra flavor. Make drink garnishes by skewering berries onto a nautical-themed drink pick.

 GIVE THEM CUPCAKES

Banana Cream Cheese Cupcakes (or Baby's First Banana Cupcakes)

Most infants love bananas, so this is the perfect cake for baby's first birthday. (If you are concerned about giving a baby too much sugar, you can cut the sugar in half; doing so will still result in a tasty cupcake!) Add a small dollop of Cream Cheese Buttercream to the cupcakes and let your baby go to town. Buttercream from head to toe is a one-year-old's rite of passage! For the rest of your guests, tint the buttercream shades of the sea and top with homemade Zissou-style cupcake picks.

MAKES 2 DOZEN CUPCAKES

What You Need:

Banana Cupcakes, recipe on page 191

Cream Cheese Buttercream, recipe on page 200

Food coloring (optional)

Cupcake picks (optional)

1. Make the Banana Cupcakes.
2. While the cupcakes cool, prepare the Cream Cheese Buttercream.
3. Divide the buttercream into two bowls and tint in two shades of aqua blue.
4. Hand-frost freestyle and create "waves" using an offset spatula (see Trophy Frosting Techniques, page 32). Top cupcakes with homemade picks. Try your hand at making ones with a yellow submarine and a Zissou-style "1."

THE VERY HUNGRY CATERPILLAR PARTY

Here's another beloved story that has all of the elements for a perfectly marvelous theme party: great colors, tasty food, and an adorable main character! It's no wonder *The Very Hungry Caterpillar* has become a go-to party theme for the under-three set. If you need some help in the crafting department (I know I did when my son was a toddler), you can find premade party packages in this theme on Etsy.com.

SET THE STAGE

- Use the wonderful art of Eric Carle as inspiration for your color palette and party decor. Cut out large leaf and fruit shapes (with a hole "bitten" out of every one of 'em) and a big yellow sun from construction paper. Tape the shapes up behind your buffet table to create a colorful backdrop, and use extra shapes as decorations. Make a large tissue paper pom-pom caterpillar to hang from the ceiling (see Get Crafty, below).

PRO-TIP

For young children's parties, remember to schedule the festivities around naptime and limit the time to two hours or less.

GET CRAFTY

Giant Pom-Pom Caterpillar

SUPPLIES

- 12 sheets of red and 50 sheets of green tissue paper (minimum)
- 1 yard of string or ribbon
- Scissors
- Construction paper
- Pipe cleaners

1. Make 5 to 7 green pom-poms for the caterpillar body and 1 red one for the head (see How to Make Tissue Paper Pom-Poms, page 146). Use construction paper and pipe cleaners to make a face on the red pom-pom (try to match Eric Carle's caterpillar). Hang each green pom-pom from the ceiling to create the caterpillar's body ("floating in mid-air") and the red one at one end for the head.

HOW TO MAKE TISSUE PAPER POM-POMS

SUPPLIES (PER POM-POM)

12 to 18 sheets of tissue paper (20 by 30 inches will make a 20-inch round pom-pom)

1 foot of string or ribbon

Scissors

- Make each pom-pom by layering 12 to 18 pieces of tissue paper. Experiment with layering to create multicolor and ombré effects.
- Accordion-fold the tissue, starting from the shorter end of the paper, in 2-inch sections. Secure the center of the accordion-folded strip by tying string or ribbon around it and tying a knot. You can leave one end of the ribbon or string long for hanging, or tie more on later. If you'd like smaller poms simply cut the accordion-folded strip into 2 to 3 pieces—secure in the center and continue.
- Trim the ends of the tissue with a soft arch, exaggerated arch, or point, depending on the look you want.
- Create the pom-pom by carefully pulling the tissue sheets, one by one, away from each other toward the center tie. Fluff and you're ready to hang your pom-pom!

ENTERTAIN THEM

- To set the stage, gather the children for a reading of *The Very Hungry Caterpillar* soon after they've arrived. Have the kids craft their own caterpillars with Popsicle sticks, pipe cleaners, colorful pom-poms, googly eyes, and glue. Send each child home with a goody bag filled with organic apple chips, fun stickers, Caterpillar coloring sheets (available on Eric-Carle.com), and a small pack of crayons, plus their make-and-take Popsicle crafts.

SERVE UP BITES & SIPS

- Serve up kid-friendly foods featured in *The Very Hungry Caterpillar*: fruit salad made with chopped apples, pears, plums, strawberries, and oranges; cheese-and-salami sandwiches cut into triangles, with a hole in each made with an apple corer or straw; small pickles; and watermelon slices—all with more caterpillar holes. Juice boxes or Martinelli's apple juice in apple-shaped glass bottles are great for young guests.

Caramel Apple Cupcakes

The Hungry Caterpillar ate his way through apples and cupcakes . . . so make yummy Caramel Apple Cupcakes! This combination of fresh apples and gooey homemade caramel is a classic, and is especially suited for events during the autumn months. The apple decor makes it perfect for this party! You can find the green wafer paper leaves for the decorative garnish at CakeDeco.com.

MAKES 2 DOZEN CUPCAKES

What You Need:

- **Caramel Sauce**, recipe on page 218
- **Apple Cupcakes**, recipe on page 194
- **Caramel Buttercream**, recipe on page 206
- 1½ cups toasted pecan halves or pieces, finely chopped
- 2 dozen pretzel sticks
- 2 dozen green wafer paper leaves

1. Make the Caramel Sauce.
2. Measure out ⅔ cup of the caramel for the buttercream and refrigerate it in a wide, shallow dish so that it cools quickly.
3. Make the Apple Cupcakes.
4. While the cupcakes cool, make the Caramel Buttercream.
5. To make your cupcakes look just like apples, scoop 1½ ounces of buttercream onto each cupcake and frost into a smooth dome (see Trophy Frosting Techniques, page 32).
6. Edge each cupcake in pecans: Grab a handful of chopped pecans. Pick up the cupcake by its liner with your other hand and carefully dip the edges of the buttercream into the pecans, lifting and turning as necessary.
7. To finish, drizzle a zigzag of the remaining caramel across the top of each cupcake (either put it in a squeeze bottle or use a small spoon).
8. Place a pretzel stick in the center of each cupcake sticking straight up (the apple's "stem") and a green wafer leaf next to it.

PRO-TIP

The Caramel Sauce can be made and stored in an airtight container for up to a week in the refrigerator. Just bring to room temp before using.

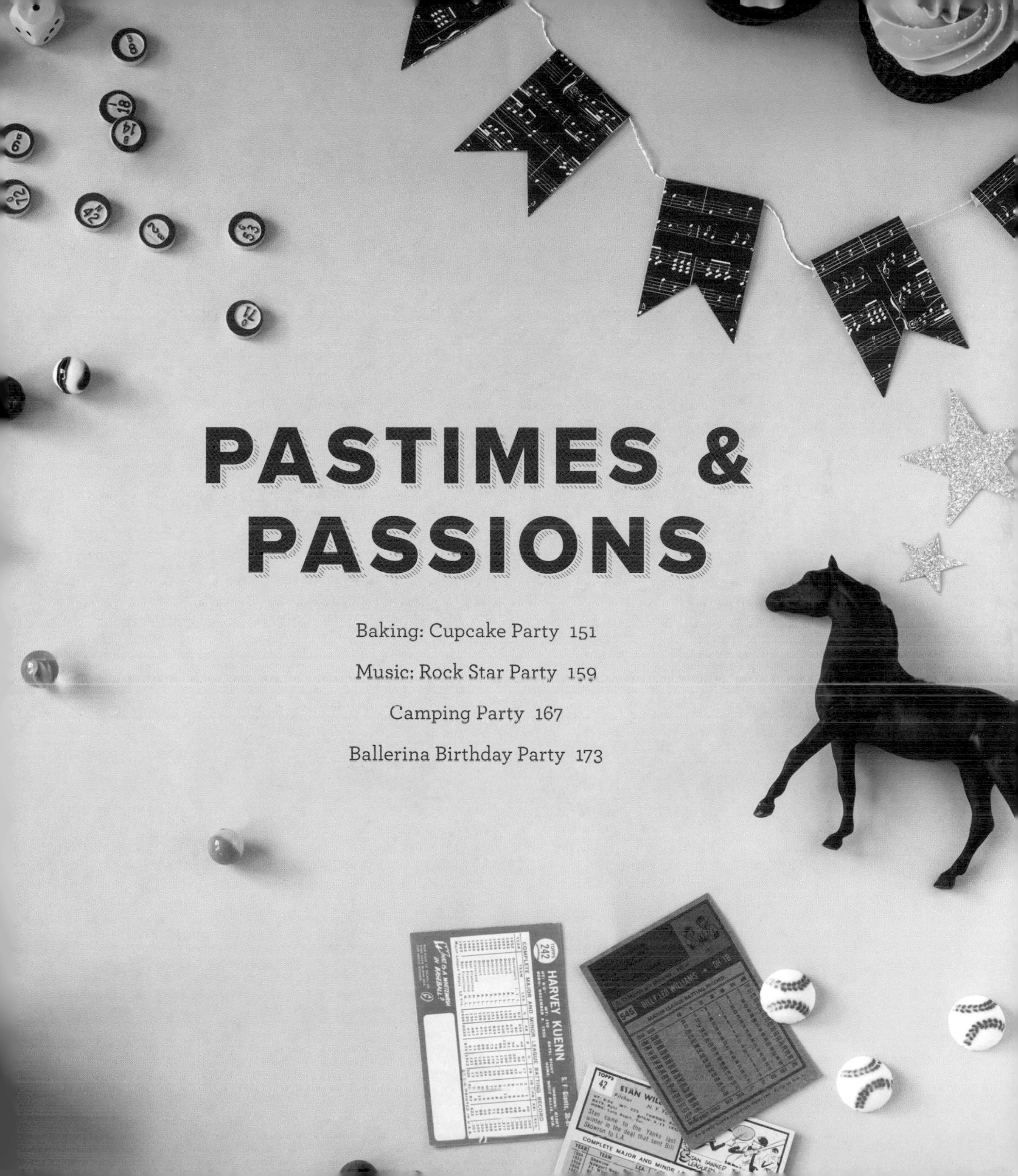

PASTIMES & PASSIONS

Some pastimes are so much fun they deserve to take center stage as the entire theme of a party. What is your guest of honor's favorite activity? Imagine a party centered around baking, painting, ballet, roller skating, knitting, golfing, hiking, swimming, or baseball; where all the decor, crafts, food, drinks, cupcakes, and entertainment are themed to the activity; all the guests take part; and everyone has a blast.

Passions make creative and fun party themes too. A passion can really be *anything*; Meyer Lemons, model airplanes, Indian textiles, Franciscan dinnerware, red wine, vintage broaches, French bulldogs . . . *I mean anything!* I once helped throw a birthday party for a good friend who's obsessed with candy, the color pink, and onions—yes, onions. She adores them and actually wrote her thesis on the sweet onion. The room was decked in pink paper pom-pom decorations (see page 146); we had a pink candy buffet; and the long farm table we dined at had a thick "runner" of Walla Walla sweet onions from end to end.

See? You can create a unique event based on just about any pastime or passion, and if the party is a birthday or special occasion, it can be truly personalized for the guest of honor. So let your mind go wild: what is the guest of honor's favorite hobby, activity, secret passion, or passing fancy? In this chapter, I've focused on some of my own most beloved pastimes and passions—baking, music, and camping—to show you how to create spectacular events.

BAKING: CUPCAKE PARTY

Baking and cooking are my lifelong passions, so this theme is my personal go-to for all kinds of parties, whether it's a girls-night-in pizza-making bash, a secret-dish potluck housewarming, or a bridal shower where everyone makes cookies or jars of jam for the couple to give as wedding favors.

It's fun to create things as a group—especially if the results are delicious. On special occasions, you can get fancy and hire an expert (or a friend, if you're lucky enough to know a professional chef or culinary whiz) for a teaching demo. For this event, I planned a special party for Chloe, a Trophy-obsessed young birthday girl, and created Chloe's Confectionery, a "bakery"—complete with cupcake-making activities—just for her.

SET THE STAGE

Go for Color

- Evoke shades of pastry icing and colors found in old-style bakeries. For this party, I went with Trophy's aqua and added tones of yellow and pink for accents. I also love the classic palette of bakery-box pink and bright white.

Decorate

- For this party, I created a bakery storefront in a friend's home, focusing on the kitchen. My goal was to make guests feel like they were walking into a sweet little bakery as they arrived and to keep that feeling going through the whole party.
- To get them excited, I created an invitation that reads more like a flyer to a bakery's grand opening than a regular invite. I printed party details on nice card stock (you can find a template in the Printables section of TrophyCupcakes.com/book) and mailed the invites in crisp aqua envelopes. A cute alternative would be to print the invitation details by hand on a recipe card and mail it in a colorful envelope.
- Be sure the wording of the invitation encourages the spirit of the "grand-opening" event, for example: "You're invited to the Grand Opening of CHLOE'S CONFECTIONERY for an afternoon of BAKE-BELIEVE."
- Every business needs a logo, and Chloe's Confectionery was no exception. You'll want to create one to place on everything from the invitation to the aprons and bakery boxes. If you don't have any graphic designer friends who can whip up something for you, visit a site like FreeLogoService.com or VistaPrint.com. Simply enter your field (for example, "bakery" for this party) and then your company name. In a matter of seconds, you'll have all kinds of logos to choose from!

- Print the logo on sticker paper (I used 2-inch round labels) and place the stickers on bakery boxes stacked high in every corner. Getting a stamp made is also a great idea—it can be used in place of stickers or in addition to them. I stamped the napkins, our vintage-inspired paper pastry bags, and the tags on sodas and other treats displayed on our "bakery counter." Style the bakery counter area to look like the genuine thing, complete with yummy baked goods (including cupcakes of course), rustic sandwiches, and old-fashioned sodas on ice (see Serve Up Bites & Sips, page 156).

- Aprons customized with your confectionery logo are adorable, not to mention handy while everyone's baking up a storm. They also make terrific take-home gifts. I created the ones for Chloe's Confectionery at MyTrickPony.com, an online shop that will take your custom design (or create a design for you) and place it on shirts, aprons, hats, linens, and other items. You can also find blank aprons at online sources such as OrientalTradingCo.com and have them embroidered locally. Or use paint pens to personalize with fun designs and guests' names. (Be sure to do this beforehand so the aprons are dry for the party.)

- Paint, print, or sketch a sign with your company name and hang it on the front door or on a wall just inside the door, that welcomes guests to the "bakery." Create a second sign to hang over the "bakery counter" in the kitchen or dining room, which will be the centerpiece of the party.

HOW MANY TO INVITE?

If the baking party is happening in your kitchen, you may need to limit the number of guests. Think about how much space your guests will realistically need, as well as baking-time restraints. If it's a kids' party, consider how many children you can supervise at one time.

Chloe

GET CRAFTY

Cupcake Liner Garlands

Have you ever decorated your kitchen for a party? What could be more fun and apropos than using cupcake liners to make your decorations? It's easy to string them together to create adorable garlands. These are fast, easy, and inexpensive garlands that really enhance the theme of a cupcake bakery in the kitchen.

SUPPLIES (PER GARLAND)

- Cupcake liners in desired sizes and colors—at least 6 dozen for each 12-foot garland
- Large needle
- 12-foot piece of heavy string, baker's twine, or narrow ribbon

1. Thread the needle with string and tie the end.
2. Pierce the middle of a cupcake liner through the bottom and thread onto the string, leaving 12 inches on the end for hanging.
3. Pierce and thread the next liner through the inside so the liners "face" each other. Add as many cupcake liners as you like, continuing to alternate, spacing evenly or grouping, depending on how full you would like your garland to be.
4. Tie a knot at the loose end of the string to secure the liners, leaving 12 inches for hanging. Repeat to make as many garlands as you like, and hang them around the party space.

ENTERTAIN THEM

- Gather everyone in the kitchen and let the entertainment begin! For Chloe's party, I preheated the oven and set out all of the ingredients ahead of time, along with measuring spoons and cups, bowls, and several copies of the recipe. As a group we made Chocolate Cupcakes (recipe on page 188), divvying up tasks as we went. I chose chocolate because it's popular and foolproof, but by all means, choose any recipe from this book that you think will work for your group. While the cupcakes were baking, we made the Vanilla Buttercream (recipe on page 198); again simple and loved by all. As always, measure and sift the confectioners' sugar ahead of time and make sure your butter is at room temperature so the buttercream whips up quickly. Take a snack break while the cupcakes cool.
- Next up is decorating. Set up the decorating station (as much as possible) before the party. For quick and easy cleanup, cover your worktable with kraft paper or a disposable tablecloth. Place at least ten kinds of sprinkles and toppings in small bowls or sturdy cupcake liners down the center of the table (enough for everyone to pass around and decorate to their hearts' content). Some of my favorites toppings

for "Decorate Your Own Cupcake" parties include white chocolate sprinkles, edible glitter, ballerina toppers, maraschino cherries, heart quins (heart-shaped candy sprinkles), and rainbow nonpareils (see Toppings Glossary, page 31). But the sky's the limit! Try crushed cookies, small candies, shaved coconut, and chopped nuts too.

- When the buttercream is prepared, divide it into at least four bowls and tint three of them with the party color or colors of your choice. Provide plenty of offset spatulas or place the buttercream in small pastry bags fitted with various tips. Fill enough for each guest to have at least one bag, so no one is ever waiting for buttercream. (For young kids, have the buttercream already whipped into an array of dazzling colors all set out in pretty bowls with offset spatulas, or in small clear-plastic pastry bags secured with rubber bands to keep the buttercream from going everywhere.)

- When the decorating is done, display the cupcakes on tiered cake plates and host an old-fashioned baking contest, with guests using cute voting sheets (visit the Printables section of TrophyCupcakes.com/book) for "Prettiest Cupcake," "Craziest Cupcake," "Best Buttercream," and "Best Sprinkles."

- Tally up the votes and, after singing "Happy Birthday" (and starting in on the sweet confections), hold an awards ceremony with ribbons for the winners. For my award ribbons, I used cupcake liners again. Print out the awards template (visit the Printables section of TrophyCupcakes.com/book) and cut out each circle with a 1- or 2-inch round punch. Glue the punched round to the center of a stack of flattened cupcake liners that have been fringed around the edges Next, using a 1- to 2-inch-wide ribbon, cut two lengths about 4 to 6 inches long. Overlap the ribbon and glue it on the center back of the cupcake liners. Trim ribbon ends with a V-cut. (See photo on the copyright page.)

- Remember all those stacked pastry boxes you used as party decor? Send them home with guests, filled with their gorgeous cupcakes. They'll also covet their custom aprons and recipe cards, including, of course, the recipe for the cupcakes you just made. You could even make favor bags with cupcake liners, mini bags of sprinkles and dragées, and pastry bag or offset spatula.

SERVE UP BITES & SIPS

- Keep the theme going with bakery-style party food, such as mini brioche sandwiches wrapped in parchment, tied with striped baker's twine, and arranged on a cookie sheet the way you'd see them in a French *boulangerie*. Serve fruit salad in individual sturdy cupcake liners (or nut cups), and adorn the table with lots of treat-filled candy jars, tiered cake plates, baskets of confections in white pastry bags, and whisks, spoons, cupcake pans, and other bakery items as props. Keep bottles of root beer and other old-fashioned sodas on ice, and make miniature ice cream floats for dessert.

Chloe's
13 birthday lane

GIVE THEM CUPCAKES

Triple Coconut Cupcakes

Although you are baking and decorating cupcakes as part of this party (see Entertain Them, page 155), Chloe is a Triple Coconut fan, and I wanted her birthday cupcakes displayed on the "bakery counter" to be extra perfect . . . so I whipped them up for her in advance.

MAKES 2 DOZEN CUPCAKES

What You Need:

Coconut Cupcakes, recipe on page 195

Coconut Buttercream, recipe on page 207

Sweetened coconut flakes

1. Make the Coconut Cupcakes.
2. While the cupcakes cool, make the Coconut Buttercream.
3. Roll the cupcakes in the coconut flakes (see Trophy Frosting Techniques, page 33). Be sure there are no clumps in your coconut before you start rolling.

SHOULD YOU BAKE FROM SCRATCH?

Normally, of course, the answer would be *yes*! But if you're baking and decorating as a party, you might want to bake—or at least prep—some things ahead of time. If your guests are young (or if you're worried about their attention spans), decide whether they'll be up for baking from scratch as well as how long you'd like the party to run.

For three- to five-year-olds, it's great to have the cupcakes, buttercream, and decorations prepared ahead of time so they can focus on decorating. For kids aged six to eight, mix the batter ahead of time (or have everything measured out and ready to mix in), so they can help you pour it into liners, and frost and decorate the results later with already-prepped buttercream. Since Chloe's guests were ten to thirteen, I chose to bake from scratch. This process takes two to three hours, so it's perfect for slumber parties and/or older kids who will stay interested throughout the whole process.

MUSIC: ROCK STAR PARTY

You don't need to play an instrument or be a karaoke legend to host a music-themed party: this theme is about music appreciation!

Pick (or have your guest of honor pick) a favorite band, musician, or musical style to celebrate. Imagine a cosmic, David Bowie–as–Ziggy Stardust theme; a neon, teased-hair Madonna-circa-1985 party; a British mod, Vespa-and-parkas bash in honor of The Who; or celebrations of Justin Bieber, Elvis Presley, or just about any iconic band or pop star. Another option is to focus on a genre, such as jazz, heavy metal, or house music—or an era, such as the 1920s, '50s, or '70s. This theme is a hit for lots of celebrations, including birthdays, graduations, Father's Day, Halloween, and bar/bat mitzvahs.

For this party, the guest of honor loves all things rock 'n' roll, so I created a Rock Star Party, complete with a make-believe band. I love to use BandNameMaker.com. Let the site choose a band name for you at random, or enter the guest of honor's name for a list of custom names. It helped me come up with "Henry and the Rock Candies" for this rock party.

SET THE STAGE

Go for Color

- Your color palette should be inspired by the musician or musical style you choose. Borrow colors from album covers, song titles, vintage music magazines and books, and music videos; for example, "Purple Haze," "Yellow Submarine," "Blue Suede Shoes," Sunny Day Real Estate's pink album. For this rock star party, I went with tried-and-true black, white, and silver.

Decorate

- Start by creating a fun "ticket" invitation (visit the Printables section of TrophyCupcakes.com/book). I used a concert ticket as inspiration, then filled in the details of the party: Come see Henry and the Rock Candies, with the date and time of the "show," along with the address. If you want to send an electronic invitation, "Golden Ticket" on PaperlessPost.com is a great alternative.

- Be sure to encourage guests to dress the part, as rockers from the celebrated era or genre, groupies, or their favorite pop icon (see Dress Your Guests, page 43). Have a friend "work the door," taking tickets and providing each guest with a mock "VIP all-access backstage pass" on a lanyard (these are easy to find online) to wear around their neck during the party. Or make your own backstage pass featuring the band name or artwork from the era of your party.

VIP
PASS
Henry and the
ROCK
CANDIES
Set the Stage — Rock 'n' Roll Swag
Get Crafty — Rock Star Party Stage
Entertain Them — Rent a Rock Star!
Serve Up Bites + Sips — Signature Rock Candy Italian Soda
Give Them Cupcakes — Triple Chocolate Rock Star Cupcakes

- Embellish your party space with rock-and-roll elements, such as lightning bolts, rock posters, and lots of musical instruments. Set up a "tattoo parlor"—a table of temporary tattoos—and get your most-inked friend to play tattoo artist. You can order them online or design custom tattoos at home with temporary tattoo paper.
- Every rock show needs a merch booth. I made custom Henry and the Rock Candies T-shirts, buttons, patches, and CD compilations featuring the same artwork from the ticket invitation, for guests to wear and/or take home.

GET CRAFTY

Rock Star Party Stage

For my rock party, I created a faux stage—the perfect backdrop for a live band or a karaoke crowd.

SUPPLIES

- Black fabric
- Method for attaching fabric (such as a staple gun)
- Spotlights
- Holiday lights
- Embellishments such as silver stars and rock posters

1. Simply tack your fabric to the wall or ceiling so it looks thick and full (like movie theater drapes) and not flat on the wall. You could also use a freestanding pole system called "pipe and drape" (available at party rental shops) to hang drapes.

2. Point a couple of spotlights at the fabric and drape the backdrop with a strand of holiday lights and couple of silver stars or rock posters.

3. It's also fun to create a "backstage" photo booth with black streamers, silver Mylar stars hanging on clear thread, and the band's name emblazoned on a banner. Include a prop table with rock star sunglasses, musical instruments, leather jackets, and wild wigs. Have a friend or photographer capture snaps of the rockers or set a digital camera with a shutter extension cable on a tripod, and let your guests go to town!

♫ ENTERTAIN THEM

- It goes without saying that you'll be playing music nonstop for this party. For the under-ten set, consider hiring a local kids' rock band (here in Seattle, The Not-Its!, Recess Monkey, and Caspar Babypants are three favorites), or make (or play) CDs of kid-rock songs, I especially love "No!" and "Here Comes Science" by They Might Be Giants. For teenagers, find out if any of their friends have a band and invite them to play. Or get a grown-up band "back together" for a reunion show. If a live band isn't in the cards, create an appropriate playlist that'll get your guests dancing.

SERVE UP BITES & SIPS

- Big-time rock stars all have backstage riders that specify *exactly* what the band wants to eat and drink in the green room. Create your own rider as the featured "menu" for the food table. Be sure to include very specific likes and dislikes: for example, a kids' party might have riders such as "green M&M's *only*" and "peanut butter sandwiches, crusts removed," while adult party riders might read "four handles of Jack Daniel's" or "domestic beer—*no* imports!" For adult parties, you may even want to go online and find a famous, over-the-top rider from a rock icon. Print it out and place it on tables around the party—your guests will be talking about it all night.

- You can also keep things very simple by providing classic "stadium foods" such as popcorn, hot dogs, and fountain drinks. Or serve favorite foods from the musical era you're celebrating. For a 1950s party, you might set up a soda fountain complete with silver dollar burgers, Elvis sandwiches (fried banana and peanut butter), and a milkshake bar . . . and don't forget The Elvis Cupcake (recipe on page 178). For a 1960s party, break out the fondue pot. If your party pays homage to a specific band or musician, research their favorite foods.

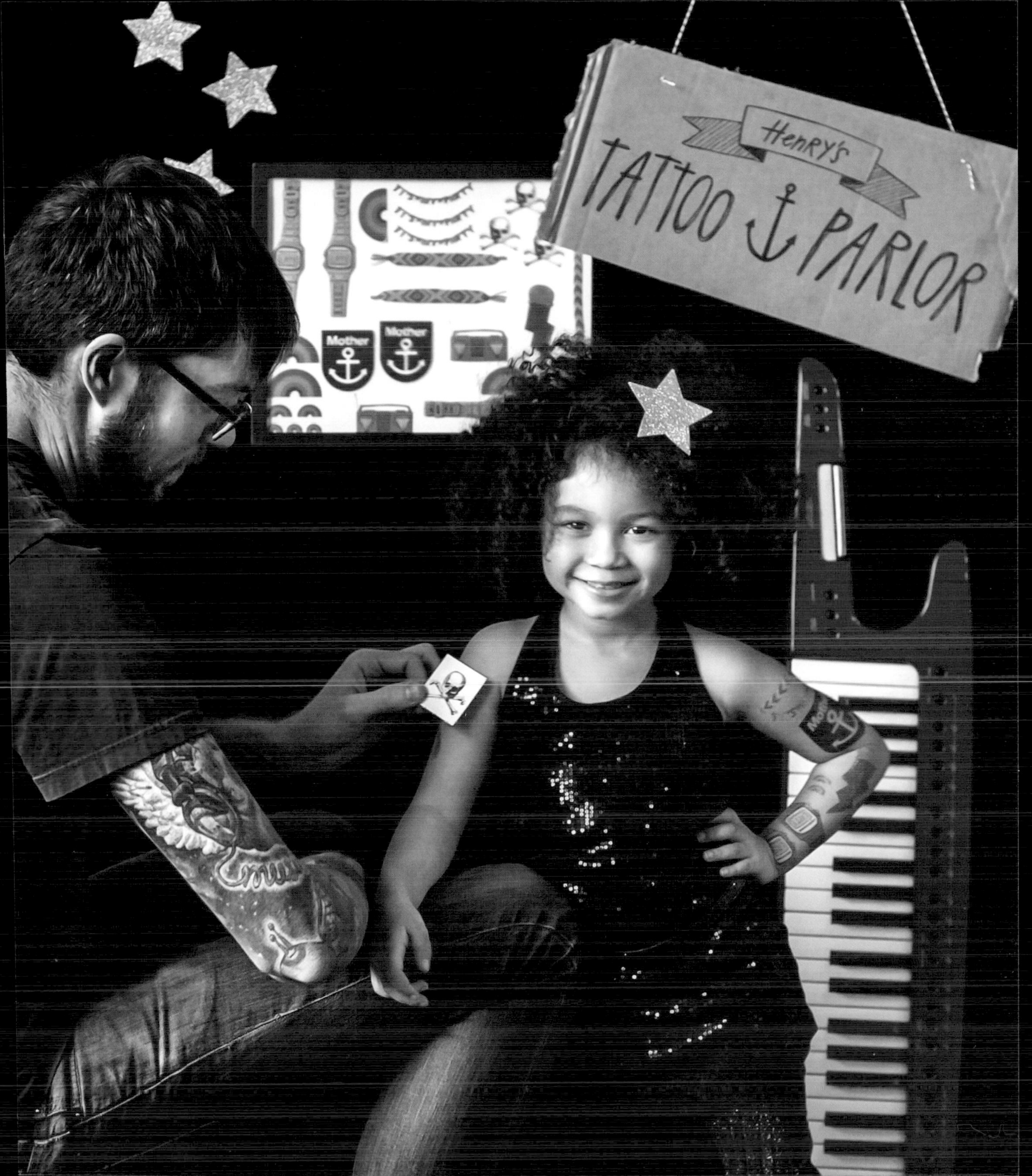
Henry's
TATTOO PARLOR
Mother
Mother

You Rock
Rock -n- Roll

GIVE THEM CUPCAKES

Triple Chocolate Rock Star Cupcakes

Trophy's classic Triple Chocolate Cupcake (see below) is the perfect canvas for a rock star party! Instead of rolling the cupcakes in French chocolate sprinkles, decorate them with rock symbols, edible glitter, and rock 'n' roll cupcake picks. For this party, I hand-piped lightning bolts and the letter "H" onto the cupcakes, then sprinkled the shapes with edible silver glitter (see Toppings Glossary, page 31) and arranged them on record sleeve "platters."

MAKES 2 DOZEN CUPCAKES

What You Need:

Chocolate Cupcakes, recipe on page 188

Chocolate Buttercream, recipe on page 208

½ recipe **Vanilla Buttercream,** for piping, recipe on page 198

Black food coloring (optional)

Clear sanding sugar

Edible silver glitter

Rock 'n' roll cupcake picks

1. Make the Chocolate Cupcakes.
2. While the cupcakes cool, make the Chocolate Buttercream and the Vanilla Buttercream. If desired, mix a small amount of food coloring with the vanilla buttercream to create a pale gray color.
3. Hand-frost the cupcakes flat with the chocolate buttercream using an offset spatula (see Trophy Frosting Techniques, page 32).
4. Edge each cupcake in clear sanding sugar and silver edible glitter (see How to Edge a Cupcake, page 31).
5. Place the vanilla buttercream in a pastry bag fitted with an Ateco tip #2 or 4. Pipe and fill in the shape or letter of your choice on each cupcake. Smooth the shape with an offset spatula, then sprinkle with glitter. For more definition, pipe around the shape in gray (or even black!) buttercream. (You can make black buttercream by adding more food coloring to the remaining vanilla buttercream.)
6. Place a cupcake pick in each cupcake.

Make Them Trophy

To make classic Trophy Triple Chocolate Cupcakes, top **Chocolate Cupcakes** with **Chocolate Buttercream** using a 1 ½-ounce scoop and roll (see page 33) in **Cacao Barry French chocolate flakes.**

CAMPING PARTY

Ah, the great outdoors! I grew up tromping through the woods with my pop, a great outdoorsman. Our pre-dawn backcountry hikes and close calls with porcupines are some of my most cherished memories. Whether you live near the mountains, desert, ocean, or lakes, there's nothing like spending a night in nature. While daytime is for games and exploration, evenings are for gathering around the campfire, telling ghost stories, and cooking food on a stick—the best kind!

Even when summer is months away, you can re-create the camping experience indoors (or outside, depending on the climate). But come summertime, there's nothing like a backyard camping party to make the kids wildly happy. Or use this theme to celebrate birthdays or Father's Day. In this case, I celebrated my young friend Huck's eighth birthday.

SET THE STAGE

Go for Color

- This theme should incorporate nature's earthy tones in classic outdoorsy textiles such as Navajo-style rugs, Pendleton blankets, and logger plaids. Try khaki, burnt sienna, navy blue, and yellow ocher or a palette of ivory, yellow, green, black, and red (like a classic Hudson's Bay blanket). You could also draw inspiration from a favorite plaid shirt.

Decorate

- Think about iconic camping accessories (binoculars, compasses) and items from the natural world, such as pinecones, logs, pine trees, birds, deer, and campfires. They all make great motifs for invitations, as well as awesome party decorations.
- Vintage or vintage-inspired camping lanterns create authentic lighting. Or make your own "lanterns" with large mason jars and candles. Firmly secure wire around the jar mouths, drop a small candle inside, and hang the jars from tree branches and fences.
- Depending on what neck of the woods you're from, procure old tree stumps and arrange them around a fire pit or campfire, along with groups of camping chairs and stools. Decorate food stations and other areas with small, round cross sections of tree stumps and branches (available at Save-On-Crafts.com).
- I also love classic national park signs—download the "Brody" font from UrbanFonts.com to re-create their great vintage look. You can also make rustic signs by painting directly on flat pieces of wood. Signs like "Camp Huck," "Mess Hall," "Campfire," "Latrines," and "S'mores" are great fun to post around the party.

GET CRAFTY

Pinecone Garlands

Pinecone garlands make a wonderful addition to this party. If you're lucky enough to live near the woods or a park that is home to conifers, you have free and easy access to pinecones. You can also buy them in craft stores.

SUPPLIES

About 12 small pinecones

Floral wire

12 feet of thick twine

Scissors

½ yard of plaid fabric in your color scheme; or old plaid shirts available at thrift shops

1. Wrap wire around the base of each pinecone and end with a small loop. String twine through the loops, positioning a pinecone every foot or so.
2. Rip or cut fabric into strips about 1 foot long by 1 to 2 inches wide.
3. Tie a strip of fabric centered between each pinecone, tied in a knot.

ENTERTAIN THEM

- Roasting hotdogs and toasting marshmallows will keep some folks occupied for hours, but it's thoughtful to arrange some lively activities for young guests. A nature scavenger hunt is a great way to exercise busy minds and restless legs. Also, don't underestimate the hours of fun a simple pup tent can provide for the kiddos.
- For all-nighter events, have guests bring their own sleeping bags for an outdoor sleepover. After the fire has died down and everyone is snuggled into their bags, screen a movie on a bedsheet hung between two tree branches. Be sure to play something outdoor-themed, such as *The Great Outdoors*, *Harry and the Hendersons*, *Mountain Family Robinson*, *The Bear*, or Yogi Bear cartoons.

Pinecone Bird Feeders

- Bird feeders are a fun make-and-take for kids. Each kid will need a large pinecone, twine, a cellophane bag, and good-size portions of peanut butter and birdseed, as well as sunflower seeds and raisins (both optional).
- Before the party, cover a picnic table to prevent peanut butter–related messes. Set large bowls of birdseed (available at most home improvement stores) in the center of the table along with separate bowls of peanut butter, raisins, and sunflower seeds.

continued

toasted
S'MORES

Tie the top of each pinecone securely with twine (with a loop for hanging) and place in baskets at each end of the table.

- At the party, have kids slather their cones in peanut butter (compostable or wooden butter knives work great), and then sprinkle, press, or roll handfuls of birdseed into the cone. Carefully add sunflower seeds and raisins in the crevices, and gently lower each pinecone into the cellophane bag using the twine loop. Guests can hang their bird feeders on a tree by their own home.

SERVE UP BITES & SIPS

- Camp food is easy to re-create with a fire pit or grill and pointy sticks. Serve hot dogs, marshmallows, hobo dinners (potatoes, carrots, onions, and—if you like—beef, pork, or veggie dogs roughly diced, salt-and-peppered, and wrapped in parchment-lined tinfoil with butter to slowly cook on the grill above the coals), and corn on the cob wrapped in tinfoil and heated near the coals. Heat a big pot of chili above the fire and serve it with melted cheddar in vintage-style enamel camp mugs alongside warm cornbread cooked in miniature cast-iron skillets. Another option is to serve traditional grilled hot dogs, hamburgers, barbecued chicken, and shish kebabs. Set up a topping station with all the fixings for guests to dress their grilled delights.
- Classic s'mores—a toasted marshmallow and a square of chocolate squished between two plain graham crackers—is a time-honored camp classic first seen in "Tramping

MARTHA AND ME

Trophy's S'mores Cupcake was created especially for none other than Martha Stewart.

Martha's staff contacted us in 2008, to "audition" our cupcakes for her show's upcoming Cupcake Week. To make sure everything went perfectly, I flew to New York and whipped up eight kinds of cupcakes in my friend's teeny, tiny Manhattan kitchen. I packaged them up for Martha and her staff to try—complete with photos of our other cupcakes.

The cupcakes were a hit, and Martha especially loved a photo we'd included of our Candied Yam Cupcake, topped with toasted marshmallow meringue. She asked if I could create a similar but not so seasonal cupcake for an upcoming April show. Naturally, I agreed. Inspired by the Candied Yam Cupcake's meringue, I dreamt up the S'mores Cupcake.

Martha called our S'mores Cupcake "utterly delicious," and it's been an ongoing Trophy favorite since it first appeared on her show on April 3, 2008. In fact, you can still find the recipe on Martha's website under "Favorite Cupcakes."

and Trailing with the Girl Scouts" in 1927. My mom was a Girl Scout leader and I grew up making and loving classic s'mores, but when I'm feeling more decadent, I like to take things up a notch with specialty flavored s'mores. My flavor experiments resulted in these two new favorites: Spicy Chocolate S'mores (vanilla bean marshmallows and organic spicy dark chocolate from TheoChocolate.com, between chocolate wafer cookies) and Nutty Toasted Coconut S'mores (toasted coconut marshmallows and organic dark chocolate between soft peanut butter cookies). With the many varieties of gourmet chocolate bars, marshmallows, and cookies, the yummy flavor combinations are endless!

TAKE THE LADIES GLAMPING!

Don't think camping parties are just for the kiddos. This theme is also fun for a ladies' night out or a bridal shower. Just glam up the details: for example, you could serve s'mores martinis or spiked hot chocolate in camp cups and watch *Dirty Dancing* under the stars!

- Create individual-serving specialty s'mores kits in vintage wood berry baskets (or green paper berry baskets) with each kit featuring a different flavor combination.

GIVE THEM CUPCAKES

S'mores Cupcakes

Nostalgic and tasty, Trophy's Chocolate Graham Cracker Cupcake topped with toasted marshmallow meringue (aka S'mores Cupcake) has been one of our most popular flavors since it was featured on *The Martha Stewart Show* in 2008 (see Martha and Me, page 170).

MAKES 2 DOZEN CUPCAKES

What You Need:

Graham Cracker Crust for S'mores Cupcakes, recipe on page 216

Chocolate Cupcakes for S'mores Cupcakes, recipe on page 189

9 ounces bittersweet chocolate

Meringue Frosting, recipe on page 199

Kitchen torch

PRO-TIP

To save time, make the crust up to a week in advance. Store in an airtight container.

1. Make the Graham Cracker Crust.
2. Make the Chocolate Cupcakes.
3. Fill the cupcake liners (with the graham cracker crusts in place) three-quarters full with the cupcake batter. Sprinkle with the reserved graham cracker mixture and chocolate. Bake until the tops of the cupcakes are firm and a cake tester inserted in the center of a middle cupcake comes out with just a few crumbs, about 20 minutes. Let the cupcakes cool for 5 minutes in the pans before removing to a rack to cool completely.
4. When the cupcakes are completely cooled, make the Meringue Frosting.
5. Place the frosting in a pastry bag fitted with a star tip (Ateco #867) and pipe a high swirl on each cupcake, then brown the meringue with a kitchen torch and serve immediately.

BALLERINA BIRTHDAY PARTY

Is ballet a favorite pastime or passion for your guest of honor? Then they'll be sure to swoon over the idea of a ballerina party. You can create a party inspired by the details of a specific performance, like Swan Lake or The Nutcracker. Or you can keep things simple, making your party all about the color pink, tulle, and pointe shoes—like we did.

SET THE STAGE

- Decorate with lots of pink and tulle, plus tutus, pointe shoes, ballerina motifs, and satin ribbons. Package a ballerina-themed invitation in a cellophane bag with pink sprinkles, a vintage ballerina cupcake topper, and a Happy Birthday tiara.

GET CRAFTY

Ballerina Tutus

- Make tutus for each guest by looping strips of tulle onto a thick satin ribbon. Look online for easy, no-sew tutu ideas and instructions. (I love the instructions and photos found on TreasuresforTots.blogspot.com; search "no-sew tutu".) Pink tulle pompom decorations hanging everywhere would also be super cute; simply swap tulle for the tissue paper in the instructions on page 146.

ENTERTAIN THEM

- Find a local ballet studio that hosts parties and have a ballet teacher lead a brief dance lesson, or invite a real ballerina from a local dance school to do a short performance and answer questions in your home. Present a gift bag to each guest that's filled with ballerina books, stickers, and trinkets galore.

SERVE UP BITES & SIPS

- Serve pink-and-white everything just like the Hello Kitty Party (page 121): tea sandwiches, dollops of shrimp salad in dainty pink cups, strawberries, raspberries, watermelon, pink soda, and pink lemonade with pink-and-white-striped straws. Drape your table copiously with ruffled pink tulle.

GIVE THEM CUPCAKES

Strawberry Lemonade Cupcakes

Strawberry Lemonade Cupcakes are our luscious lemon cakes filled with strawberry jam and topped with a pretty pink ruffle of oh-so-strawberry buttercream. It's the perfect complement to any girly affairs and the ruffled top paired with a ballerina cupcake topper will delight savvy ballerinas with big expectations.

MAKES 2 DOZEN CUPCAKES

What You Need:

Lemon Cupcakes, recipe on page 183

Strawberry Buttercream, recipe on page 209

1½ cups strawberry jam, for filling

Apple corer

Pink sanding sugar

Ballerina cupcake toppers (optional)

1. Make the Lemon Cupcakes.
2. While the cupcakes cool, make the Strawberry Buttercream.
3. Core the center of each cooled cupcake. Fill the well with strawberry jam (see How to Fill a Cupcake, page 179).
4. Frost each cupcake with a vintage ruffle (see Be a Piping Pro, page 36).
5. Sprinkle with pink sanding sugar, and adorn with classic ballerina cupcake toppers!

RECIPES: BATTERS, BUTTERCREAMS & MORE

All of the recipes plus yummy ideas for mixing and matching flavors

Give them cupcakes! You've seen all kinds of cupcake ideas throughout this book, and this is where you'll find the complete individual recipes that make up each and every one of them. This comprehensive section provides every detail you'll need to whip up dreamy cupcake batters, buttercreams (and other frostings), fillings, crusts, and toppings.

I recommend bookmarking three pages for any cupcake you're making: the page that introduces the cupcake idea, and the pages with the recipe for the batter and the frosting—so you can flip back and forth easily.

We offer up some more mix and match ideas on pages 178, but don't be afraid to create your own yummy combinations!

Give Me More Cupcakes!

There are many recipes in this book that you can mix and match, or tweak slightly, to create more of Trophy's most popular flavors, such as the following.

SALTED CARAMEL CUPCAKES

Top **Chocolate Cupcakes** (page 188) with a low swirl of **Caramel Buttercream** (page 206), using Ateco tip #828, drizzle with **Caramel Sauce** (page 218), and sprinkle with ***fleur de sel***.

VANILLA CHOCOLATE CUPCAKES

Top **Vanilla Cupcakes** (page 182) with **Chocolate Buttercream** (page 208) in a Trophy Wave style, using Ateco tip #847, and sprinkle with **white nonpareils**.

CHOCOLATE CREAM CHEESE CUPCAKES

Top **Chocolate Cupcakes** (page 188) with a low swirl of **Cream Cheese Buttercream** (page 200), using Ateco tip #828, and sprinkle with **mini chocolate chips**.

SNOWBALL CUPCAKES

Top **Chocolate Cupcakes** (page 188) with **Coconut Buttercream** (page 207), using a 1½-ounce scoop, and roll (see page 33) in **pink coconut flakes** (see Tint Your Own Sanding Sugar and Coconut Flakes, page 33).

CHOCOLATE MACAROON CUPCAKES

Top **Coconut Cupcakes** (page 195) with **Chocolate Buttercream** (page 208), using a 1½-ounce scoop, and roll (see page 33) in **toasted coconut flakes** (made by placing an even layer of a coconut flakes on a cookie sheet in a 300-degree oven for 5 to 10 minutes, stirring frequently until golden brown. Cool before using.

CHOCOLATE PEANUT BUTTER CUPCAKES

Top **Chocolate Cupcakes** (page 188) with a Trophy Wave of **Peanut Butter Buttercream** (page 210), using Ateco tip #847, and sprinkle the center with **crushed peanuts** and ***fleur de sel***.

THE ELVIS CUPCAKE

Top **Hummingbird Cupcakes** (page 190) with a low swirl of **Peanut Butter Buttercream** (page 210), using Ateco tip #828, drizzle with **honey** and sprinkle with **yellow nonpareils** and **clear sanding sugar**.

For the following three flavors, make ½ batches of the buttercreams (and meringue frosting).

NEAPOLITAN CUPCAKES

Top **Chocolate Cupcakes** (page 188) with a low swirl of **Strawberry Buttercream** (page 209) and a smaller swirl of **Vanilla Buttercream** (page 198) atop that, using Ateco tip #828, sprinkle with **pastel confetti sprinkles** and **chocolate flakes** (page 28), and top with a **maraschino cherry**.

FLUFFERNUTTER CUPCAKES

Top **Vanilla Cupcakes** (page 182) with a low swirl of **Peanut Butter Buttercream** (page 210) and a smaller swirl of **Meringue Frosting** (page 199) atop that, using Ateco tip #828, and sprinkle the center with **crushed peanuts**.

PEANUT BUTTER AND JELLY CUPCAKES

Fill **Vanilla Cupcakes** (page 182) with thick strawberry jam (see page 179) and top with a low swirl of **Peanut Butter Buttercream** (page 210) and then a smaller swirl on top of that of **Strawberry Buttercream** (page 209), using Ateco tip #828, and sprinkle with **pastel confetti sprinkles**.

Even More Trophy Classics!!

With simple tweaks to our Vanilla Buttercream (page 198), you can create more Trophy classics in your own kitchen.

CHOCOLATE NUTELLA CUPCAKES

Add 1 cup Nutella with the vanilla extract. Make our **Chocolate Nutella Cupcakes** by hand-frosting our **Chocolate Cupcakes** (page 188) with this **Nutella Buttercream** and edging them with **chopped candied hazelnuts** (see How to Edge a Cupcake, page 31).

SNICKERDOODLE CUPCAKES

Add **1 teaspoon cinnamon** with the vanilla extract. To make our dreamy **Snickerdoodle Cupcakes**, sprinkle 1 teaspoon equal parts cinnamon and sugar atop **Vanilla Cupcakes** (page 182) just before baking. Frost the cupcakes with a Trophy Wave of **Cinnamon Buttercream**, using Ateco tip # 847, and sprinkle lightly with **cinnamon** and **clear sanding sugar**.

Adding even a simple filling can increase the wow factor of any cupcake. Here's how with a few recipes to get you started.

HOW TO FILL A CUPCAKE: Use an apple corer (like we do), cupcake corer, melon baller, or teaspoon to remove the center of the cake. Make a well that's big enough to hold about 1 tablespoon of filling. Don't break through the bottom of the cake or crust. Save the cupcake centers to sprinkle on ice cream or make mini trifles!

CHOCOLATE RASPBERRY CUPCAKES

Make **Raspberry Buttercream** by adding 1½ cups thick **raspberry jam** with the vanilla to the **Vanilla Buttercream** recipe (page 198). Puree jam or preserves in a food processor if they contain large pieces of fruit. Fill **Chocolate Cupcakes** (page 188) with **raspberry jam**, then top with a Vintage Ruffle of the buttercream, using Ateco petal tip #127, and garnish with a **fresh raspberry** and **clear sanding sugar**.

RASPBERRY LEMONADE CUPCAKES

Fill **Lemon Cupcakes** (page 183) with thick **raspberry jam**. Top with a Vintage Ruffle of **Raspberry Buttercream** (see above), using Ateco petal tip #127, and garnish with a **fresh raspberry** and **clear sanding sugar**.

RASPBERRY MACAROON CUPCAKES

(Inspired by the Hostess Tiger Tail!) Top **Coconut Cupcakes** (page 195) with a 1½-ounce scoop of **Raspberry Buttercream** (see above), roll in **shaved coconut** (see page 33), and drizzle with **Simple Raspberry Sauce** (see below).

PRO-TIP: Make **Simple Raspberry Sauce** by heating 1½ cups raspberry jam over medium heat until thin. Let cool, place in a squeeze bottle, and drizzle on cupcakes (or ice cream).

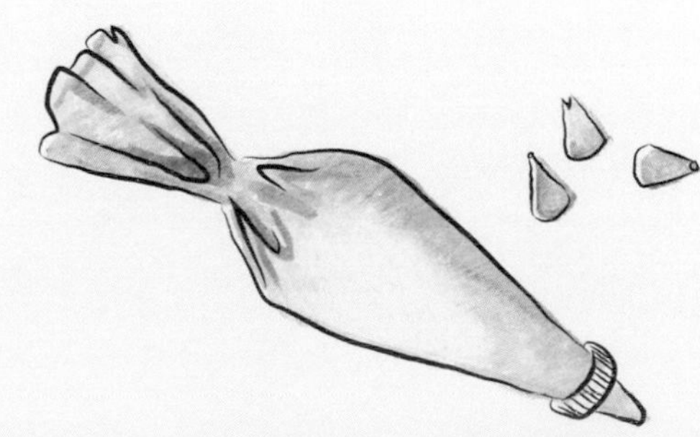

CUPCAKE BATTERS

Pink Champagne Cupcakes

MAKES 2 DOZEN CUPCAKES

2 cups cake flour (not self-rising)

1½ cups all-purpose flour

1 tablespoon plus ½ teaspoon baking powder

1 teaspoon salt

⅔ cup champagne

⅔ cup half-and-half

¼ teaspoon red food coloring

1½ cups (3 sticks) unsalted butter, at room temperature

2⅓ cups sugar

3 eggs

1. Preheat the oven to 350 degrees F. Line two 12-cup muffin pans with cupcake liners and set aside.

2. In a large bowl, sift together the cake flour, all-purpose flour, baking powder, and salt. Set aside.

3. Combine the champagne, half-and-half, and food coloring in a large measuring cup with a spout. Set aside.

4. Combine the butter and sugar in the bowl of a stand mixer fitted with the paddle attachment and beat them at low speed until the mixture is smooth and creamy, about 1 minute if the butter is soft. If the butter is cool, it will take longer. Add the eggs one at a time, mixing well and scraping the bowl after each addition, and waiting until all traces of each egg have disappeared before adding the next one.

5. Add the dry ingredients in 3 parts, alternating with adding the wet ingredients in 2 parts. Keep the mixer at the lowest speed, and mix each time just until the ingredients are combined. When everything has been added, scrape the bowl and paddle one more time, and stir the batter just until it's smooth. Let the batter rest for 15 minutes and stir gently before using.

6. Fill the cupcake liners three-quarters full and bake until the tops of the cupcakes are firm and a cake tester inserted into the center of a middle cupcake comes out with just a few crumbs, about 20 minutes. Let the cupcakes cool for 5 minutes in the pans before removing to a rack to cool completely.

Vanilla Cupcakes

MAKES 2 DOZEN CUPCAKES

2½ cups all-purpose flour

1 cup cake flour (not self-rising)

2 teaspoons baking powder

1¼ teaspoons salt

1 cup milk

½ cup plus 3 tablespoons half-and-half

1 tablespoon plus 1 teaspoon vanilla extract

1 cup (2 sticks) unsalted butter, at room temperature

2¾ cups sugar

3 eggs

1. Preheat the oven to 350 degrees F. Line two 12-cup muffin pans with cupcake liners and set aside.

2. In a large bowl, sift together the all-purpose flour, cake flour, baking powder, and salt. Set aside.

3. Combine the milk, half-and-half, and vanilla in a large measuring cup with a spout. Set aside.

4. Combine the butter and sugar in the bowl of a stand mixer fitted with the paddle attachment and beat them at low speed until the mixture is smooth and creamy, about 1 minute if the butter is soft. If the butter is cool, it will take longer. Add the eggs one at a time, mixing well and scraping the bowl after each addition, and waiting until all traces of each egg have disappeared before adding the next one.

5. Add the dry ingredients in 3 parts, alternating with adding the wet ingredients in 2 parts. Keep the mixer at the lowest speed, and mix each time just until the ingredients are combined. When everything has been added, scrape the bowl and paddle one more time, and stir the batter just until it's smooth. Let the batter rest for 15 minutes and stir gently before using.

6. Fill the cupcake liners three-quarters full and bake until the tops of the cupcakes are firm and a cake tester inserted in the center of a middle cupcake comes out with just a few crumbs, about 20 minutes. The cupcakes should still be very pale and turn golden only around the edges. Let the cupcakes cool for 5 minutes in the pans before removing to a rack to cool completely.

Lemon Cupcakes

MAKES 2 DOZEN CUPCAKES

- 1 tablespoon plus 1 teaspoon lemon zest
- ¼ cup freshly squeezed lemon juice (from 2 medium lemons)
- 2¼ cups cake flour (not self-rising)
- 1¼ cups all-purpose flour
- 1 tablespoon plus 1 teaspoon baking powder
- 1¼ teaspoons salt
- ½ teaspoon baking soda
- 1 cup buttermilk
- 1 cup (2 sticks) unsalted butter, at room temperature
- 2¼ cups sugar
- 3 eggs
- ½ cup sour cream

1. Preheat the oven to 350 degrees F. Line two 12-cup muffin pans with cupcake liners and set aside.

2. Zest 2 lemons and set zest aside. Juice 1/4 cup lemon juice and set aside.

3. In a large bowl, sift together the cake flour, all-purpose flour, baking powder, salt, and baking soda. Set aside.

4. Combine the buttermilk and lemon juice in a large measuring cup with a spout. Set aside.

5. Combine the lemon zest, butter, and sugar in the bowl of a stand mixer fitted with the paddle attachment and beat them at low speed until the mixture is smooth and creamy, about 1 minute if the butter is soft. If the butter is cool, it will take longer. Add the eggs one at a time, mixing well and scraping the bowl after each addition, and waiting until all traces of each egg have disappeared before adding the next one. Add the sour cream and mix until smooth.

6. Add the dry ingredients in 3 parts, alternating with adding the wet ingredients in 2 parts. Keep the mixer at the lowest speed, and mix each time just until the ingredients are combined. When everything has been added, scrape the bowl and paddle one more time, and stir the batter just until it's smooth. Let the batter rest for 15 minutes and stir gently before using.

7. Fill the cupcake liners three-quarters full and bake until the tops of the cupcakes are firm and a cake tester inserted in the center of a middle cupcake comes out with just a few crumbs, about 20 minutes. Let the cupcakes cool for 5 minutes in the pans before removing to a rack to cool completely.

Red Velvet Cupcakes

MAKES 2 DOZEN CUPCAKES

- 2 cups cake flour (not self-rising)
- 1¾ cups all-purpose flour
- ⅓ cup plus 1 tablespoon cocoa powder
- 2 teaspoons baking powder
- ¾ teaspoon salt
- 1½ cups buttermilk
- ¾ cup vegetable oil
- 2 tablespoons red food coloring
- 2 teaspoons vanilla extract
- ½ cup (1 stick) plus 2 tablespoons unsalted butter, at room temperature
- 2¼ cups sugar
- 3 eggs
- 1 teaspoon baking soda
- 1 teaspoon white vinegar

1. Preheat the oven to 350 degrees F. Line two 12-cup muffin pans with cupcake liners and set aside.

2. In a large bowl, sift together the cake flour, all-purpose flour, cocoa powder, baking powder, and salt. Set aside.

3. Combine the buttermilk, oil, food coloring, and vanilla in a large measuring cup with a spout. Set aside.

4. Combine the butter and sugar in the bowl of a stand mixer fitted with the paddle attachment and beat them at low speed for 1 minute, then increase the speed to medium and beat until the mixture becomes a smooth dough, about 1 more minute.

5. With the mixer at its lowest speed, add the eggs one at a time, mixing well and scraping the bowl after each addition, and waiting until all traces of each egg have disappeared before adding the next one. When all the eggs have been added, scrape the bowl and continue to beat until the mixture is smooth and creamy, about 1 minute. Do not overmix.

6. Add the dry ingredients in 3 parts, alternating with adding the wet ingredients in 2 parts. Keep the mixer at the lowest speed, and mix each time just until the ingredients are combined. When adding the second half of the wet ingredients, combine the baking soda and vinegar in a small cup and add it to the batter along with the liquids. When everything has been added, scrape the bowl and paddle one more time, and stir the batter just until it's smooth. Let the batter rest for 15 minutes and stir gently before using.

7. Fill the cupcake liners three-quarters full and bake until the tops of the cupcakes are firm and a cake tester inserted in the center of a middle cupcake comes out with just a few crumbs, about 20 minutes. Let the cupcakes cool for 5 minutes in the tins before removing to a rack to cool completely.

Crème Brûlée Cupcakes

MAKES 10 CUPCAKES

- ¾ cup plus 1½ tablespoons all-purpose flour
- ⅓ cup cake flour (not self-rising)
- ⅔ teaspoon baking powder
- ½ teaspoon salt
- ⅓ cup milk
- ¼ cup half-and-half
- 1½ teaspoons vanilla extract
- 5½ tablespoons unsalted butter, at room temperature
- ¾ cup plus 2½ tablespoons sugar
- 1 egg
- 2½ cups (1 batch) Lavender Pastry Cream (page 214)
- 1 cup granulated sugar
- Kitchen torch

1. In a large bowl, sift together the all-purpose flour, cake flour, baking powder, and salt. Set aside.

2. Combine the milk, half-and-half, and vanilla in a measuring cup with a spout. Set aside.

3. Combine the butter and sugar in the bowl of a stand mixer fitted with the paddle attachment and beat them at low speed until the mixture is smooth and creamy, about 1 minute if the butter is soft. If the butter is cool, it will take longer. Add the eggs one at a time, mixing well and scraping the bowl after each addition, and waiting until all traces of each egg have disappeared before adding the next one.

4. Add the dry ingredients in 3 parts, alternating with adding the wet ingredients in 2 parts. Keep the mixer at the lowest speed, and mix each time just until the ingredients are combined. When everything has been added, scrape the bowl and paddle one more time, and stir the batter just until it's smooth. Set the batter aside.

5. Preheat the oven to 350 degrees F. Line 10 cups in a 12-cup muffin pan with 2 cupcake liners each and set aside while you make the Lavender Pastry Cream.

6. Use all the cupcake batter to fill the double-lined muffin cups three-quarters full. Level the top of the batter with the back of a spoon, if necessary. Place a biscuit cutter or mousse ring on top of each cupcake well. Using a small portion scoop with a trigger or squeeze handle, divide the pastry cream evenly between all 10 cups (about 1/4 cup in each). You want to do this slowly and carefully (if you drop a big blob of pastry cream onto the batter, it may sink). If you don't have a portion scoop, use two small spoons to divide the pastry cream: take a scoop of pastry cream with one spoon, and use the other spoon to push it evenly over the cupcake batter. When all the pastry cream is divided onto the batter, smooth the tops if necessary. The pastry cream level will be about 1 inch above the top of the cupcake pan with the biscuit ring holding it in place.

continued

7. Bake the cupcakes for 25 to 30 minutes. The pastry cream will rise to the top of the biscuit cutter as the cake rises; don't worry if a little spills over.

8. The best way to tell if the cupcakes are done is to remove the pan from the oven at about 25 minutes to see if any cupcake batter has risen to the top (it tends to push the pastry cream out of the way). If it has, insert a cake tester in the center of a middle of a cupcake: it should come out with just a few crumbs. If no cake is peeking out, place the cupcakes back into the oven for 5 more minutes. At this point, they should be done. The pastry cream will keep them from overbaking.

9. Let the cupcakes cool completely before removing the biscuit rings. Use a small metal spatula to carefully remove the cupcakes from the pan.

10. To serve, carefully remove the outer cupcake liner from each cupcake, leaving the clean inner liner still attached. Place the cupcakes on a sheet pan or a fireproof work surface. Sprinkle each one with about a teaspoon of granulated sugar, and use a kitchen torch to caramelize it by holding the flame quite close to the top of each cupcake, moving it slowly to melt all the sugar. Let the cupcakes sit for at least 5 minutes to let the caramel harden. Serve on a plate with a spoon so that your guests can experience the ultimate pleasure of cracking the top. You can caramelize the tops up to 1 hour before serving. Any longer than that, and the caramel will become watery.

Lime Cupcakes

MAKES 2 DOZEN CUPCAKES

- 1 tablespoon plus 1 teaspoon lime zest
- ¼ cup freshly squeezed lime juice (from about 2 medium limes)
- 2¼ cups cake flour (not self-rising)
- 1¼ cups all-purpose flour
- 1 tablespoon plus 1 teaspoon baking powder
- 1¼ teaspoons salt
- ½ teaspoon baking soda
- 1 cup buttermilk
- 1 cup (2 sticks) unsalted butter, at room temperature
- 2¼ cups sugar
- 3 eggs
- ½ cup sour cream

1. Preheat the oven to 350 degrees F. Line two 12-cup muffin pans with cupcake liners and set aside.

2. Zest the limes and set zest aside. Juice 1/4 cup lime juice and set aside.

3. In a large bowl, sift together the cake flour, all-purpose flour, baking powder, salt, and baking soda. Set aside.

4. Combine the buttermilk and lime juice in a large measuring cup with a spout. Set aside.

5. Combine the lime zest, butter, and sugar in the bowl of a stand mixer fitted with the paddle attachment and beat them at low speed until the mixture is smooth and creamy, about 1 minute if the butter is soft. If the butter is cool, it will take longer. Add the eggs one at a time, mixing well and scraping the bowl after each addition, and waiting until all traces of each egg have disappeared before adding the next one. Add the sour cream and mix until smooth.

6. Add the dry ingredients in 3 parts, alternating with adding the wet ingredients in 2 parts. Keep the mixer at the lowest speed, and mix each time just until the ingredients are combined. When everything has been added, scrape the bowl and paddle one more time, and stir the batter just until it's smooth. Let the batter rest for 15 minutes and stir gently before using.

7. Fill the cupcake liners three-quarters full and bake until the tops of the cupcakes are firm and a cake tester inserted in the center of a middle cupcake comes out with just a few crumbs, about 20 minutes. Let the cupcakes cool for 5 minutes in the pans before removing to a rack to cool completely.

Chocolate Cupcakes

MAKES 2 DOZEN CUPCAKES

3 cups all-purpose flour

1¼ cups cocoa powder

2½ teaspoons baking powder

1½ teaspoons baking soda

¾ teaspoon salt

3 eggs

1½ cups milk

¾ cup canola oil

1 tablespoon vanilla extract

2¾ cups sugar

1 cup boiling water

1. Preheat the oven to 350 degrees F. Line two 12-cup muffin pans with cupcake liners and set aside.

2. In a large bowl, sift together the flour, cocoa powder, baking powder, baking soda, and salt. Set aside.

3. Combine the eggs, milk, oil, and vanilla in the bowl of a stand mixer fitted with the paddle attachment. Add the sugar and dry ingredients. Blend at low speed, then increase the speed to medium and mix until the batter is completely smooth, about 2 minutes. Remove the bowl from the stand and add the boiling water and stir with a wooden spoon, carefully so that it doesn't splash, until the batter is smooth again. It will be thin. Let the batter rest for 15 minutes and stir gently before using.

4. Fill the cupcake liners three-quarters full and bake until the tops of the cupcakes are firm and a cake tester inserted in the center of a middle cupcake comes out with just a few crumbs, about 20 minutes. Let the cupcakes cool for 5 minutes in the pans before removing to a rack to cool completely.

Chocolate Cupcakes for S'mores Cupcakes

MAKES 2 DOZEN CUPCAKES

- 2 cups all-purpose flour
- ¾ cup plus 1 teaspoon cocoa powder
- 1½ teaspoons baking powder
- 1 teaspoon baking soda
- ½ teaspoon salt
- 2 eggs
- 1 cup milk
- ½ cup canola oil
- 2 teaspoons vanilla extract
- 1¾ cups plus 2 tablespoons sugar
- ⅔ cup boiling water

1. Be sure to first prepare the Graham Cracker Crust for S'mores Cupcakes on page 216.

2. Increase the oven temperature to 350 degrees F.

3. In a large bowl, sift together the flour, cocoa powder, baking powder, baking soda, and salt. Set aside.

4. Combine the eggs, milk, oil, and vanilla in the bowl of a stand mixer fitted with the paddle attachment. Add the sugar and dry ingredients. Blend at low speed, then increase the speed to medium and mix until the batter is completely smooth, about 2 minutes. Remove the bowl from the stand and add the boiling water and stir with a wooden spoon, carefully so that it doesn't splash, until the batter is smooth again. It will be thin. Let the batter rest for 15 minutes and stir gently before using.

5. Fill the cupcake liners (with the graham cracker crusts in place) three-quarters full with the cupcake batter. Sprinkle with the reserved graham cracker mixture and chocolate. Bake until the tops of the cupcakes are firm and a cake tester inserted in the center of a middle cupcake comes out with just a few crumbs, about 20 minutes. Let the cupcakes cool for 5 minutes in the pans before removing to a rack to cool completely.

Hummingbird Cupcakes

MAKES 2 DOZEN CUPCAKES

- 3 cups all-purpose flour
- 1¾ teaspoons baking soda
- ½ teaspoon ground cinnamon
- ½ teaspoon salt
- 3 eggs
- ¾ cup plus 2 tablespoons canola oil
- 1¾ teaspoons vanilla extract
- ½ teaspoon coconut extract
- 1½ cups sugar
- ¼ cup plus 1 tablespoon firmly packed light brown sugar
- 1½ cups mashed ripe banana (about 3 bananas)
- ¾ cup drained crushed pineapple
- 1½ cups sweetened flaked coconut

1. Preheat the oven to 350 degrees F. Line two 12-cup muffin pans with cupcake liners and set aside.

2. In a large bowl, sift together the flour, baking soda, cinnamon, and salt. Set aside.

3. Combine the eggs, oil, and vanilla and coconut extracts in the bowl of a stand mixer fitted with the paddle attachment and beat them at low speed until the mixture is smooth and creamy, about 1 minute. Add the sugars and mix to blend. Add the bananas, pineapple, and coconut, and mix on low speed to break up the bananas. Add the dry ingredients and mix on low speed for 30 seconds to incorporate, then increase the speed to medium and beat just until combined.

4. Fill the cupcake liners three-quarters full, and bake until the tops of the cupcakes are firm and golden, and a cake tester inserted in the center of a middle cupcake comes out with just a few crumbs, about 20 minutes. Let the cupcakes cool for 5 minutes in the pans before removing to a rack to cool completely.

Banana Cupcakes

MAKES 2 DOZEN CUPCAKES

- 2 cups cake flour (not self-rising)
- 1½ cups all-purpose flour
- 1¾ teaspoons baking powder
- 1 teaspoon baking soda
- ½ teaspoon salt
- 1 cup buttermilk
- 1 tablespoon vanilla extract
- ½ cup (1 stick) plus 6 tablespoons unsalted butter, at room temperature
- 1½ cups sugar
- 3 eggs
- 1½ cups mashed ripe banana (about 3 bananas)

1. Preheat the oven to 350 degrees F. Line two 12-cup muffin pans with cupcake liners and set aside.

2. In a large bowl, sift together the cake flour, all-purpose flour, baking powder, baking soda, and salt. Set aside.

3. Combine the buttermilk and vanilla in a large measuring cup with a spout. Set aside.

4. Combine the butter and sugar in the bowl of a stand mixer fitted with the paddle attachment and beat them at low speed until the mixture is smooth and creamy, about 1 minute if the butter is soft. If the butter is cool, it will take longer. Add the eggs one at a time, mixing well and scraping the bowl after each addition, and waiting until all traces of each egg have disappeared before adding the next one.

5. Add the bananas and stir until smooth. Add the dry ingredients in 3 parts, alternating with adding the wet ingredients in 2 parts. Keep the mixer at the lowest speed, and mix each time just until the ingredients are combined. When everything has been added, scrape the bowl and paddle one more time, and stir the batter just until it's smooth. Let the batter rest for 15 minutes and stir gently before using.

6. Fill the cupcake liners three-quarters full and bake until the tops of the cupcakes are firm and a cake tester inserted in the center of a middle cupcake comes out with just a few crumbs, about 20 minutes. Let the cupcakes cool for 5 minutes in the pans before removing to a rack to cool completely.

Strawberry Cupcakes

MAKES 2 DOZEN CUPCAKES

3 cups all-purpose flour

1 cup cake flour (not self-rising)

2½ teaspoons baking powder

1½ teaspoons salt

⅔ cup milk

⅔ cup half-and-half

1 tablespoon vanilla extract

1 cup (2 sticks) unsalted butter, at room temperature

2 cups sugar

3 eggs

½ cup smooth strawberry jam

1 cup chopped fresh or frozen strawberries

1. Preheat the oven to 350 degrees F. Line two 12-cup muffin pans with cupcake liners and set aside.

2. In a large bowl, sift together the all-purpose flour, cake flour, baking powder, and salt. Set aside.

3. Combine the milk, half-and-half, and vanilla in a large measuring cup with a spout. Set aside.

4. Combine the butter and sugar in the bowl of a stand mixer fitted with the paddle attachment and beat them at low speed until the mixture is smooth and creamy, about 1 minute if the butter is soft. If the butter is cool, it will take longer. Add the eggs one at a time, mixing well and scraping the bowl after each addition, and waiting until all traces of each egg have disappeared before adding the next one. Add the jam and mix until smooth.

5. Add the dry ingredients in 3 parts, alternating with adding the wet ingredients in 2 parts. Keep the mixer at the lowest speed, and mix each time just until the ingredients are combined. When everything has been added, scrape the bowl and paddle one more time, add the strawberries, and stir the batter just until it's smooth. Let the batter rest for 15 minutes and stir gently before using.

6. Fill the cupcake liners three-quarters full and bake until the tops of the cupcakes are firm and a cake tester inserted in the center of a middle cupcake comes out with just a few crumbs, about 20 minutes. Let the cupcakes cool for 5 minutes in the pans before removing to a rack to cool completely.

Orange and Almond Cupcakes

MAKES 2 DOZEN CUPCAKES

2 large organic oranges

½ cup (1 stick) unsalted butter

2¼ cups almond flour (such as Bob's Red Mill)

1 teaspoon baking powder

6 eggs

1¼ cups sugar

1 tablespoon rose water

1. When you're ready to make the cupcakes (or a day or two in advance), start by boiling the oranges in a large pot of water for 2 hours. Use a pot that is large enough so the oranges float. As they boil, they will bob around so that they cook evenly. Keep an eye on them and add water to the pot as needed. When the oranges have finished cooking, use tongs or a slotted spoon to remove them from the water, and let them cool for 30 minutes. Note: If you boil the oranges in advance, store them for up to 2 days in the refrigerator in an airtight container. Bring to room temperature before pureeing into the batter.

2. Preheat the oven to 350 degrees F. Line two 12-cup muffin pans with cupcake liners and set aside.

3. Melt the butter in small saucepan and set it aside to cool.

4. Whisk together the almond flour and baking powder in a large bowl until combined. Set aside.

5. Combine the eggs, sugar, and rose water in the bowl of a food processor and blend until smooth. Remove the hard stems from the oranges (if they have them) and then add the whole oranges and the melted butter to the processor and blend until smooth. Pour the orange mixture into the dry ingredients and stir until the batter is smooth.

6. Fill the cupcake liners almost to the top and bake until the tops of the cupcakes are firm and a cake tester inserted in the center of a middle cupcake comes out clean, about 30 minutes. Let the cupcakes cool for 10 minutes in the pans before removing to a rack to cool completely.

Apple Cupcakes

MAKES 2 DOZEN CUPCAKES

3 Granny Smith apples, peeled, cored, and quartered

2¼ cups sugar, divided

2 tablespoons freshly squeezed lemon juice (from 1 medium lemon)

2 teaspoons ground cinnamon, divided

3½ cups all-purpose flour

1 tablespoon baking powder

1 teaspoon ground nutmeg

1 teaspoon salt

¼ cup plus 3 tablespoons canola oil

¼ cup freshly squeezed orange juice (from 1 medium orange)

½ cup (1 stick) unsalted butter, at room temperature

3 eggs

2 teaspoons vanilla extract

1. Preheat the oven to 350 degrees F. Line two 12-cup muffin pans with cupcake liners and set aside.

2. Place an apple quarter flat side down on a cutting board. Slice it lengthwise into 4 or 5 slices, then slice it across about 5 times. Put the diced apple in a medium bowl and repeat with the remaining apple quarters. Add ¼ cup of the sugar, the lemon juice, and 1 teaspoon of the cinnamon to the apples and mix well. Set aside.

3. In a large bowl, sift together the flour, baking powder, nutmeg, salt, and remaining 1 teaspoon cinnamon. Set aside.

4. Combine the oil and orange juice in a large measuring cup with a spout. Set aside.

5. Combine the butter and remaining 2 cups sugar in the bowl of a stand mixer fitted with the paddle attachment and beat them at low speed until the mixture is smooth and creamy, about 1 minute if the butter is soft. If the butter is cool, it will take longer. Add the eggs one at a time, mixing well and scraping the bowl after each addition, and waiting until all traces of each egg have disappeared before adding the next one. Add the vanilla and mix to incorporate.

6. Add the dry ingredients in 3 parts, alternating with the wet ingredients in 2 parts. Keep the mixer at the lowest speed, and mix each time just until the ingredients are combined. When everything has been added, scrape the bowl and paddle one more time, and stir the batter just until it's smooth. Add the diced apple and any accumulated juices, and stir to incorporate.

7. Fill the cupcake liners three-quarters full and bake until the tops of the cupcakes are firm and a cake tester inserted in the center of a middle cupcake comes out with just a few crumbs, about 20 minutes. Let the cupcakes cool for 5 minutes in the pans before removing to a rack to cool completely.

Coconut Cupcakes

MAKES 2 DOZEN CUPCAKES

1½ cups cake flour (not self-rising)

1 cup all-purpose flour

2⅛ teaspoons baking powder

½ teaspoon salt

1½ teaspoons coconut extract

1 teaspoon vanilla extract

1⅓ cups coconut milk (whisk before measuring)

¾ cup plus 2 tablespoons unsalted butter, at room temperature

2 cups sugar

4 eggs

1½ cups sweetened coconut flakes

1. Preheat the oven to 350 degrees F. Line two 12-cup muffin pans with cupcake liners and set aside.

2. In a large bowl, sift together the cake flour, all-purpose flour, baking powder, and salt. Set aside.

3. Combine the coconut and vanilla extracts and coconut milk in a large measuring cup with a spout. Set aside.

4. Combine the butter and sugar in the bowl of a stand mixer fitted with the paddle attachment and beat them at low speed until the mixture is smooth and creamy, about 1 minute if the butter is soft. If the butter is cool, it will take longer. Add the eggs one at a time, mixing well and scraping the bowl after each addition, and waiting until all traces of each egg have disappeared before adding the next one. Add the coconut flakes and stir just to incorporate.

5. Add the dry ingredients in 3 parts, alternating with the wet ingredients in 2 parts. Keep the mixer at the lowest speed, and mix each time just until the ingredients are combined. When everything has been added, scrape the bowl and paddle one more time, and stir the batter just until it's smooth. Let the batter rest for 15 minutes and stir gently before using.

6. Fill the cupcake liners three-quarters full and bake until the tops of the cupcakes are firm and a cake tester inserted in the center of a middle cupcake comes out with just a few crumbs, about 20 minutes. The cupcakes should still be very pale and turn golden only around the edges. Let the cupcakes cool for 5 minutes in the pans before removing to a rack to cool completely.

BUTTERCREAM & FROSTINGS

Pink Champagne Buttercream

MAKES ABOUT 7 CUPS

3 cups (6 sticks) unsalted butter, at room temperature

6 cups confectioners' sugar, sifted

¼ cup plus 1 tablespoon champagne

2 teaspoons vanilla extract

¼ teaspoon salt

Red food coloring

1. In a stand mixer fitted with the paddle attachment, cream the butter. Start with the mixer at the lowest speed, then gradually increase the speed, using a rubber spatula to scrape the bowl as needed, until the butter is light in color, perfectly smooth, and makes a slapping sound as it hits the sides of the bowl. If the butter is soft, this should only take 30 seconds, but if the butter is cool, it can take a couple of minutes.

2. Add the sugar, 1 cup at a time, and mix at the lowest speed until it's fully incorporated before adding the next cup. When all the sugar has been added, scrape the paddle and the bottom and sides of the bowl. Add the champagne, vanilla, salt, and a drop or two of food coloring (we make ours very light pink, but you can always add more for a darker color), and beat them at low speed for 15 seconds. Increase the speed to as high as you can without making a mess and whip the buttercream until the mixture is perfectly smooth, creamy, and light, about 5 minutes. Stop the mixer once or twice to scrape the bowl and paddle, then continue beating. At first the buttercream will appear to soften, then it will stiffen and increase in volume.

3. Use right away, or store in an airtight container for up to a week in the refrigerator. When you're ready to use it, let the buttercream come to room temperature, then put it back in the stand mixer and use the paddle attachment to beat it until it's creamy and stiff again.

Vanilla Buttercream

MAKES ABOUT 7 CUPS

3 cups (6 sticks) unsalted butter, at room temperature

6 cups confectioners' sugar, sifted

2 teaspoons vanilla extract

¼ teaspoon salt

1. In a stand mixer fitted with the paddle attachment, cream the butter. Start with the mixer at the lowest speed, then gradually increase the speed, using a rubber spatula to scrape the bowl as needed, until the butter is light in color, perfectly smooth, and makes a slapping sound as it hits the sides of the bowl. If the butter is soft, this should only take 30 seconds, but if the butter is cool, it can take a couple of minutes.

2. Add the sugar, 1 cup at a time, and mix at the lowest speed until it's fully incorporated before adding the next cup. When all the sugar has been added, scrape the paddle and the bottom and sides of the bowl. Add the vanilla and salt, and beat them at low speed for 15 seconds. Increase the speed to as high as you can without making a mess and whip the buttercream until the mixture is perfectly smooth, creamy, and light, about 5 minutes. Stop the mixer once or twice to scrape the bowl and paddle, then continue beating. At first the buttercream will appear to soften, then it will stiffen and increase in volume.

3. Use right away, or store in an airtight container for up to a week in the refrigerator. When you're ready to use it, let the buttercream come to room temperature, then put it back in the stand mixer and use the paddle attachment to beat it until it's creamy and stiff again.

Meringue Frosting

MAKES ABOUT 7 CUPS

6 egg whites

1½ cups sugar

½ teaspoon cream of tartar

1½ teaspoons vanilla extract

1. Combine the egg whites, sugar, and cream of tartar in the heatproof bowl of a stand mixer. Set the bowl over a saucepan with simmering water (do not let the water touch the bottom of the bowl). Use an oven mitt to hold the handle of the bowl with one hand while you constantly whisk the egg white mixture until the sugar is dissolved and the whites are hot to the touch, about 4 minutes. Transfer the bowl to the stand and use the whisk attachment to beat the mixture, starting on low speed and gradually increasing to high speed, until stiff, glossy peaks form and the meringue has cooled, 5 to 7 minutes. Add the vanilla and whisk just to incorporate. Use immediately.

Rum Meringue Frosting

MAKES ABOUT 7 CUPS

6 egg whites

1½ cups sugar

½ teaspoon cream of tartar

1½ tablespoons rum

1 tablespoon rum extract

1. Combine the egg whites, sugar, and cream of tartar in the heatproof bowl of a stand mixer. Set the bowl over a saucepan with simmering water (do not let the water touch the bottom of the bowl). Use an oven mitt to hold the handle of the bowl with one hand while you constantly whisk the egg white mixture until the sugar is dissolved and the whites are hot to the touch, about 4 minutes. Transfer the bowl to the stand and use the whisk attachment to beat the mixture, starting on low speed and gradually increasing to high speed, until stiff, glossy peaks form and the meringue has cooled, 5 to 7 minutes. Add the rum and rum extract and whisk just to incorporate. Use immediately.

Cream Cheese Buttercream

MAKES ABOUT 6 CUPS

24 ounces (three 8-ounce packages) cream cheese, at room temperature

1½ cups (3 sticks) unsalted butter, at room temperature

3 cups plus 3 tablespoons confectioners' sugar, sifted

2 teaspoons vanilla extract

1. In a stand mixer fitted with the paddle attachment, beat the cream cheese. Start with the mixer at the lowest speed, then gradually increase the speed, using a rubber spatula to scrape the bowl as needed, until the cheese is perfectly smooth and creamy. Scrape the cream cheese into a small bowl and set aside.

2. Next, cream the butter. Start with the mixer at the lowest speed, then gradually increase the speed, using a rubber spatula to scrape the bowl as needed, until the butter is light in color, perfectly smooth, and makes a slapping sound as it hits the sides of the bowl. If the butter is soft, this should only take 30 seconds, but if the butter is cool, it can take a couple of minutes.

3. Add the sugar, 1 cup at a time, and mix at the lowest speed until it's fully incorporated before adding the next cup. When all the sugar has been added, scrape the paddle and the bottom and sides of the bowl. Add the vanilla and beat it at low speed for 15 seconds. Increase the speed to as high as you can without making a mess and whip the buttercream until the mixture is perfectly smooth, creamy, and light, about 5 minutes. Stop the mixer once or twice to scrape the bowl and paddle, then continue beating. At first the buttercream will appear to soften, then it will stiffen and increase in volume.

4. Scrape the bowl and paddle again, then add the whipped cream cheese. Beat the mixture at the lowest speed for 30 seconds to combine, then increase the speed to medium and beat for 30 seconds to lighten the buttercream.

5. Use right away, or store in an airtight container for up to a week in the refrigerator. When you're ready to use it, let the buttercream come to room temperature, then put it back in the stand mixer and use the paddle attachment to beat it until it's creamy and stiff again.

Tequila Lime Buttercream

MAKES ABOUT 7 CUPS

3 teaspoons of lime zest (about 2 medium limes)

6 tablespoons freshly squeezed lime juice (from about 3 medium limes)

3 cups (6 sticks) unsalted butter, at room temperature

6 cups confectioners' sugar, sifted

6 tablespoons tequila

2 teaspoons lime oil

1. Zest the limes and set zest aside. Juice limes and set aside.

2. In a stand mixer fitted with the paddle attachment, cream the butter. Start with the mixer at the lowest speed, then gradually increase the speed, using a rubber spatula to scrape the bowl as needed, until the butter is light in color, perfectly smooth, and makes a slapping sound as it hits the sides of the bowl. If the butter is soft, this should only take 30 seconds, but if the butter is cool, it can take a couple of minutes.

3. Add the sugar, 1 cup at a time, and mix at the lowest speed until it's fully incorporated before adding the next cup. When all the sugar has been added, scrape the paddle and the bottom and sides of the bowl. Add the tequila, lime juice and zest, and lime oil, and beat them at low speed for 15 seconds. Increase the speed to as high as you can without making a mess and whip the buttercream until the mixture is perfectly smooth, creamy, and light, about 5 minutes. Stop the mixer once or twice to scrape the bowl and paddle, then continue beating. At first the buttercream will appear to soften, then it will stiffen and increase in volume.

4. Use right away, or store in an airtight container for up to a week in the refrigerator. When you're ready to use it, let the buttercream come to room temperature if possible, then put it back in the stand mixer and use the paddle attachment to beat it until it's creamy and stiff again.

Coconut Rum Buttercream

MAKES ABOUT 7 CUPS

3 cups (6 sticks) unsalted butter, at room temperature

6 cups confectioners' sugar, sifted

¼ cup rum (we use Sailor Jerry)

2 teaspoons vanilla extract

1½ teaspoons coconut extract

¼ teaspoon salt

1. In a stand mixer fitted with the paddle attachment, cream the butter. Start with the mixer at the lowest speed, then gradually increase the speed, using a rubber spatula to scrape the bowl as needed, until the butter is light in color, perfectly smooth, and makes a slapping sound as it hits the sides of the bowl. If the butter is soft, this should only take 30 seconds, but if the butter is cool, it can take a couple of minutes.

2. Add the sugar, 1 cup at a time, and mix at the lowest speed until it's fully incorporated before adding the next cup. When all the sugar has been added, scrape the paddle and the bottom and sides of the bowl. Add the rum, vanilla and coconut extracts, and salt, and beat them at low speed for 15 seconds. Increase the speed to as high as you can without making a mess and whip the buttercream until the mixture is perfectly smooth, creamy, and light, about 5 minutes. Stop the mixer once or twice to scrape the bowl and paddle, then continue beating. At first the buttercream will appear to soften, then it will stiffen and increase in volume.

3. Use right away, or store in an airtight container for up to a week in the refrigerator. When you're ready to use it, let the buttercream come to room temperature, then put it back in the stand mixer and use the paddle attachment to beat it until it's creamy and stiff again.

Espresso Buttercream

MAKES ABOUT 7 CUPS

3 cups (6 sticks) unsalted butter, at room temperature

6 cups confectioners' sugar, sifted

½ cup very strong espresso shots, cooled, or ¾ cup instant espresso coffee (such as Medaglia D'Oro) dissolved in ½ cup hot water, cooled

1 tablespoon plus 1 teaspoon vanilla extract

½ teaspoon salt

1. In a stand mixer fitted with the paddle attachment, cream the butter. Start with the mixer at the lowest speed, then gradually increase the speed, using a rubber spatula to scrape the bowl as needed, until the butter is light in color, perfectly smooth, and makes a slapping sound as it hits the sides of the bowl. If the butter is soft, this should only take 30 seconds, but if the butter is cool, it can take a couple of minutes.

2. Add the sugar, 1 cup at a time, and mix at the lowest speed until it's fully incorporated before adding the next cup. When all the sugar has been added, scrape the paddle and the bottom and sides of the bowl. Add the cooled espresso, vanilla, and salt, and mix slowly so that the espresso doesn't splash. At first the mixture will break and appear curdled, but the buttercream will come back together as it whips. When the buttercream looks smooth again, scrape the bowl and paddle, then increase the speed to as high as you can without making a mess and whip the buttercream until the mixture is perfectly smooth, creamy, and light, about 5 minutes. Stop the mixer once or twice to scrape the bowl and paddle, then continue beating. At first the buttercream will appear to soften, then it will stiffen and increase in volume.

3. Use right away, or store in an airtight container for up to a week in the refrigerator. When you're ready to use it, let the buttercream come to room temperature, then put it back in the stand mixer and use the paddle attachment to beat it until it's creamy and stiff again.

PRO-TIP

If you don't have a great espresso maker at home, purchase about 4 strong shots from your local coffeehouse (measure out ½ cup). If you're using instant espresso, put it in a cup, add the hot water, stir to dissolve, and set aside to cool.

Strawberry Cream Cheese Buttercream

MAKES ABOUT 7 CUPS

24 ounces (three 8-ounce packages) cream cheese, at room temperature

1½ cups (3 sticks) unsalted butter, at room temperature

3 cups plus 3 tablespoons confectioners' sugar, sifted

⅔ cup thick strawberry jam

1 teaspoon vanilla extract

1. In a stand mixer fitted with the paddle attachment, beat the cream cheese. Start with the mixer at the lowest speed, then gradually increase the speed, using a rubber spatula to scrape the bowl as needed, until the cheese is perfectly smooth and creamy. Scrape the cream cheese into a small bowl and set aside.

2. Next, cream the butter. Start with the mixer at its lowest speed, then gradually increase the speed, using a rubber spatula to scrape the bowl as needed, until the butter is light in color, perfectly smooth, and makes a slapping sound as it hits the sides of the bowl. If the butter is soft, this should only take 30 seconds, but if the butter is cool, it can take a couple of minutes.

3. Add the sugar, 1 cup at a time, and mix at the lowest speed until it's fully incorporated before adding the next cup. When all the sugar has been added, scrape the paddle and the bottom and sides of the bowl. Add the jam and vanilla and beat them at low speed for 15 seconds. Increase the speed to as high as you can without making a mess and whip the buttercream until the mixture is perfectly smooth, creamy, and light, about 5 minutes. Stop the mixer once or twice to scrape the bowl and paddle, then continue beating. At first the buttercream will appear to soften, then it will stiffen and increase in volume.

4. Scrape the bowl and paddle again, then add the whipped cream cheese. Beat the mixture at the lowest speed for 30 seconds to combine, then increase the speed to medium and beat for 30 seconds to lighten the buttercream.

5. Use right away, or store in an airtight container for up to a week in the refrigerator. When you're ready to use it, let the buttercream come to room temperature, then put it back in the stand mixer and use the paddle attachment to beat it until it's creamy and stiff again.

Rose Water Buttercream

MAKES ABOUT 3½ CUPS

1½ cups (3 sticks) unsalted butter, at room temperature

3 cups confectioners' sugar, sifted

2 to 3 tablespoons rose water

Pinch of salt

1. In a stand mixer fitted with the paddle attachment, cream the butter. Start with the mixer at the lowest speed, then gradually increase the speed, using a rubber spatula to scrape the bowl as needed, until the butter is light in color, perfectly smooth, and makes a slapping sound as it hits the sides of the bowl. If the butter is soft, this should only take 30 seconds, but if the butter is cool, it can take a couple of minutes.

2. Add the sugar, 1 cup at a time, and mix at the lowest speed until it's fully incorporated before adding the next cup. When all the sugar has been added, scrape the paddle and the bottom and sides of the bowl. Add the rose water and salt, and beat them at low speed for 15 seconds. Increase the speed to as high as you can without making a mess and whip the buttercream until the mixture is perfectly smooth, creamy, and light, about 5 minutes. Stop the mixer once or twice to scrape the bowl and paddle, then continue beating. At first the buttercream will appear to soften, then it will stiffen and increase in volume.

3. Use right away, or store in an airtight container for up to a week in the refrigerator. When you're ready to use it, let the buttercream come to room temperature, then put it back in the stand mixer and use the paddle attachment to beat it until it's creamy and stiff again.

Caramel Buttercream

MAKES ABOUT 7 CUPS

3 cups (6 sticks) unsalted butter, at room temperature

6 cups confectioners' sugar, sifted

⅔ cup Caramel Sauce (page 218)

1½ teaspoons vanilla extract

¼ teaspoon salt

1. In a stand mixer fitted with the paddle attachment, cream the butter. Start with the mixer at the lowest speed, then gradually increase the speed, using a rubber spatula to scrape the bowl as needed, until the butter is light in color, perfectly smooth, and makes a slapping sound as it hits the sides of the bowl. If the butter is soft, this should only take 30 seconds, but if the butter is cool, it can take a couple of minutes.

2. Add the sugar, 1 cup at a time, and mix at the lowest speed until it's fully incorporated before adding the next cup. When all the sugar has been added, scrape the paddle and the bottom and sides of the bowl. Add the caramel sauce, vanilla, and salt, and beat them at low speed for 15 seconds. Increase the speed to as high as you can without making a mess and whip the buttercream until the mixture is perfectly smooth, creamy, and light, about 5 minutes. Stop the mixer once or twice to scrape the bowl and paddle, then continue beating. At first the buttercream will appear to soften, then it will stiffen and increase in volume.

3. Use right away, or store in an airtight container for up to a week in the refrigerator. When you're ready to use it, let the buttercream come to room temperature, then put it back in the stand mixer and use the paddle attachment to beat it until it's creamy and stiff again.

Coconut Buttercream

MAKES ABOUT 7 CUPS

- 3 cups (6 sticks) unsalted butter, at room temperature
- 6 cups confectioners' sugar, sifted
- 2 teaspoons vanilla extract
- 1½ teaspoons coconut extract
- ¼ teaspoon salt

1. In a stand mixer fitted with the paddle attachment, cream the butter. Start with the mixer at the lowest speed, then gradually increase the speed, using a rubber spatula to scrape the bowl as needed, until the butter is light in color, perfectly smooth, and makes a slapping sound as it hits the sides of the bowl. If the butter is soft, this should only take 30 seconds, but if the butter is cool, it can take a couple of minutes.

2. Add the sugar, 1 cup at a time, and mix at the lowest speed until it's fully incorporated before adding the next cup. When all the sugar has been added, scrape the paddle and the bottom and sides of the bowl. Add the vanilla and coconut extracts and salt, and beat them at low speed for 15 seconds. Increase the speed to as high as you can without making a mess and whip the buttercream until the mixture is perfectly smooth, creamy, and light, about 5 minutes. Stop the mixer once or twice to scrape the bowl and paddle, then continue beating. At first the buttercream will appear to soften, then it will stiffen and increase in volume.

3. Use right away, or store in an airtight container for up to a week in the refrigerator. When you're ready to use it, let the buttercream come to room temperature, then put it back in the stand mixer and use the paddle attachment to beat it until it's creamy and stiff again.

Chocolate Buttercream

MAKES ABOUT 6 CUPS

13 ounces bittersweet chocolate (60 percent or more cacao), chopped (see Use Trophy-Worthy Ingredients, page 26)

2¼ cups (4½ sticks) unsalted butter, at room temperature

3 cups confectioners' sugar, sifted

2½ teaspoons vanilla extract

¼ teaspoon salt

1. Make a double boiler to gently melt the chocolate by setting a small stainless steel bowl over the top of a small saucepan filled with a couple of inches of water over low heat. (Make sure the bottom of the bowl doesn't touch the water.) Use a rubber spatula to stir the chocolate occasionally and scrape the sides of the bowl so the chocolate doesn't burn. When it's almost completely melted, remove the bowl from the pan and continue stirring until all the chocolate has melted. Set the bowl aside and let the chocolate cool until it's just slightly warm.

2. In a stand mixer fitted with the paddle attachment, cream the butter. Start with the mixer at the lowest speed, then gradually increase the speed, using a rubber spatula to scrape the bowl as needed, until the butter is light in color, perfectly smooth, and makes a slapping sound as it hits the sides of the bowl. If the butter is soft, this should only take 30 seconds, but if the butter is cool, it can take a couple of minutes.

3. Add a third of the creamed butter to the melted chocolate and use a rubber spatula to fold the mixture together well, scraping the sides and bottom of the bowl; set aside.

4. Add the sugar to the remaining butter in the mixer, 1 cup at a time, and mix at the lowest speed until it's fully incorporated before adding the next cup. When all the sugar has been added, scrape the paddle and the bottom and sides of the bowl. Add the chocolate mixture, vanilla, and salt, and beat at low speed for 15 seconds. Increase the speed to as high as you can without making a mess and whip the buttercream until the mixture is perfectly smooth, creamy, and light, about 5 minutes. Stop the mixer once or twice to scrape the bowl and paddle, then continue beating. At first the buttercream will appear to soften, then it will stiffen and increase in volume.

5. Use right away, or store in an airtight container for up to a week in the refrigerator. When you're ready to use it, let the buttercream come to room temperature, then put it back in the stand mixer and use the paddle attachment to beat it until it's creamy and stiff again.

Strawberry Buttercream

MAKES ABOUT 7½ CUPS

- 3 cups (6 sticks) unsalted butter, at room temperature
- 6 cups confectioners' sugar, sifted
- 1½ cups smooth, thick strawberry jam (or pureed preserves, to taste)
- 2 teaspoons vanilla extract
- ¼ teaspoon salt

1. In a stand mixer fitted with the paddle attachment, cream the butter. Start with the mixer at the lowest speed, then gradually increase the speed, using a rubber spatula to scrape the bowl as needed, until the butter is light in color, perfectly smooth, and makes a slapping sound as it hits the sides of the bowl. If the butter is soft, this should only take 30 seconds, but if the butter is cool, it can take a couple of minutes.

2. Add the sugar, 1 cup at a time, and mix at the lowest speed until it's fully incorporated before adding the next cup. When all the sugar has been added, scrape the paddle and the bottom and sides of the bowl. Add the jam, vanilla, and salt, and beat them at low speed for 15 seconds. Increase the speed to as high as you can without making a mess and whip the buttercream until the mixture is perfectly smooth, creamy, and light, about 5 minutes. Stop the mixer once or twice to scrape the bowl and taste the buttercream. Add more jam to taste if needed, then continue beating. At first the buttercream will appear to soften, then it will stiffen and increase in volume.

3. Use right away, or store in an airtight container for up to a week in the refrigerator. When you're ready to use it, let the buttercream come to room temperature, then put it back in the stand mixer and use the paddle attachment to beat it until it's creamy and stiff again.

Peanut Butter Buttercream

MAKES ABOUT 4 CUPS

- 1¼ cups (2½ sticks) unsalted butter, at room temperature
- 2½ cups confectioners' sugar, sifted
- 1 cup creamy natural peanut butter
- ¾ teaspoon vanilla extract
- ¼ teaspoon salt

1. In a stand mixer fitted with the paddle attachment, cream the butter. Start with the mixer at the lowest speed, then gradually increase the speed, using a rubber spatula to scrape the bowl as needed, until the butter is light in color, perfectly smooth, and makes a slapping sound as it hits the sides of the bowl. If the butter is soft, this should only take 30 seconds, but if the butter is cool, it can take a couple of minutes.

2. Add the sugar, 1 cup at a time, and mix at the lowest speed until it's fully incorporated before adding the next cup. When all the sugar has been added, scrape the paddle and the bottom and sides of the bowl. Add the peanut butter, vanilla, and salt, and beat them at low speed for 15 seconds. Increase the speed to as high as you can without making a mess and whip the buttercream until the mixture is perfectly smooth, creamy, and light, about 5 minutes. Stop the mixer once or twice to scrape the bowl and paddle, then continue beating. At first the buttercream will appear to soften, then it will stiffen and increase in volume.

3. Use right away, or store in an airtight container for up to a week in the refrigerator. When you're ready to use it, let the buttercream come to room temperature, then put it back in the stand mixer and use the paddle attachment to beat it until it's creamy and stiff again.

EXTRAS

Pie Crust Rounds and Garnishes

MAKES ENOUGH FOR 2 DOZEN 2-INCH CUPCAKE CRUST ROUNDS AND 2 DOZEN 1-INCH GARNISHES OR AN 8-INCH DOUBLE CRUST PIE

¾ cup (1½ sticks) cold unsalted butter

3 tablespoons cold water

1½ teaspoons sugar (plus more for sprinkling on crust garnishes, if making)

¾ teaspoon salt

1¾ cups plus 2 tablespoons cake flour (not self-rising)

Half-and-half or milk, for brushing the garnishes

1. Preheat the oven to 400 degrees F. Line two sheet pans with parchment paper and set aside.

2. Put the bowl and paddle attachment of a stand mixer in the refrigerator. Slice each stick of butter lengthwise and then across into 8 pieces, then refrigerate the butter. Put the cold water in a small cup, add the sugar and salt, stir to dissolve, then put it in the refrigerator and chill for about 30 minutes.

3. Remove the bowl, paddle, butter, and water mixture from the refrigerator. Sift the flour into the bowl, then position the bowl into the stand. Add the cold butter pieces and mix at the lowest speed until they are the size of peas. Slowly add the cold water mixture, just until it's incorporated and a dough just starts to come together. If the dough won't hold together, add a little more cold water, just a teaspoon at a time. Be careful not to overmix.

4. Form the dough into 2 flattened discs, wrap them in plastic, and refrigerate them for at least 1 hour.

5. After the dough has been refrigerated for at least 1 hour, roll it out on a lightly floured surface until it's no more than ¼ inch thick. Use a 2-inch round cookie cutter to cut out 2 dozen pieces of dough from one flattened disc (these will be for the bottom crust of the cupcakes) and use a 1¼-inch round cookie cutter to cut out another 2 dozen pieces from the other flattened disc for the cupcake garnishes.

6. Place the 2-inch dough rounds on one of the prepared sheet pans and put it in the refrigerator. Place the smaller dough circles on the other sheet pan, brush them with a little half-and-half or milk, then sprinkle them with sugar. Bake them until they're puffed and crisp, about 11 minutes. Transfer them to a wire rack to cool.

7. Remove the sheet pan of pie crusts from the refrigerator. Use a fork to prick them a couple of times to keep them from puffing too much when they bake. Bake them until they feel firm but are still pale, about 9 minutes. Let them cool on the pan for 5 minutes.

PRO-TIP

Unbaked pie dough can be wrapped and stored in the refrigerator for up to 4 days and in the freezer for up to 3 months. Baked crusts can be stored in an airtight container for up to 3 days.

Lemon Curd

MAKES ABOUT 1 CUP

- 5 tablespoons plus 1 teaspoon freshly squeezed lemon juice (from 3 medium lemons)
- 2 eggs
- 2 egg yolks (save the whites for the Meringue Frosting, page 199)
- ½ cup sugar
- 2 tablespoons unsalted butter
- 2 teaspoons heavy cream
- ¾ teaspoon vanilla extract
- Pinch of salt

1. Bring the lemon juice to a boil in a small saucepan over medium heat, then remove from the heat and set it aside.

2. In a small bowl, whisk together the eggs and yolks, then add the sugar and lemon juice and whisk well to combine. Set a small strainer or sieve over a small bowl, and set next to the stove. Pour the lemon mixture into a small, nonreactive (stainless steel, ceramic, or nonstick) saucepan and cook over medium heat, whisking constantly, until the mixture gets thick and bubbly, 3 to 5 minutes. Remove the pan from the heat and add the butter, cream, vanilla, and salt, and whisk until smooth.

3. Pour the hot lemon curd through the prepared strainer. Use a rubber spatula to push the curd through and scrape the underside of the strainer (a lot of the curd will cling to it). Discard what remains in the strainer. Place a piece of plastic wrap directly on the surface of the lemon curd and refrigerate it until it's cold and set, about 2 hours. Lemon curd can be stored in an airtight container in the refrigerator for up to a week.

Lavender Pastry Cream

MAKES ABOUT 2½ CUPS

1½ cups heavy cream

1½ cups half-and-half

1½ tablespoons dried lavender

6 egg yolks

¾ cup sugar

3 tablespoons cornstarch

Pinch of salt

1. Put the heavy cream, half-and-half, and lavender in a small saucepan over medium heat and bring the mixture to a boil. Immediately remove the pan from the heat, cover it with a piece of aluminum foil, and let the cream steep for 15 minutes.

2. Meanwhile, combine the egg yolks and sugar in a medium bowl and whisk until smooth. Sift the cornstarch into the mixture, add the salt, and whisk until perfectly smooth.

3. When the cream has finished steeping, set a mesh sieve over a medium saucepan and pour the hot cream through it to remove the lavender. Temper the egg mixture by slowly adding about 1 cup of the hot cream to the eggs while whisking constantly, then pour the egg mixture into the saucepan that has the remaining cream in it, and whisk well.

4. Set the pan over medium heat and cook, whisking constantly, until the pastry cream gets thick (like mayonnaise) and begins to bubble. Let it boil for 30 seconds, again whisking constantly. It should be thick, smooth, and glossy. As soon as it is ready, pour it into a clean bowl.

Caramelized Pineapple

MAKES 1 GENEROUS CUP

- ¼ cup (½ stick) unsalted butter
- 1 cup firmly packed light brown sugar
- One 20-ounce can crushed pineapple, thoroughly drained

1. Melt the butter in a large saucepan over medium heat. Add the sugar and stir well to combine. Simmer until the mixture becomes a smooth, thick syrup and the sugar has melted, 2 to 3 minutes.

2. Add the pineapple and stir to combine. Reduce the heat to medium-low and let the mixture simmer, stirring occasionally to prevent burning, until most of the liquid has evaporated and the sauce has turned a deep caramel color, about 10 minutes. Thoroughly drain the pineapple in a strainer.

3. Let the pineapple cool completely before using it. If you make it ahead, you can store it in an airtight container for up to a week in the refrigerator. Bring to room temperature before spooning into cupcake liners (or use with Piña Colada Cupcakes on page 94).

Brown Sugar Caramel

MAKES ABOUT 2¾ CUPS

- 5 tablespoons unsalted butter, cut into 10 pieces
- 1⅓ cups light brown sugar
- 7 tablespoons plus 1¼ cups heavy cream, divided
- 5 tablespoons rum
- ¼ teaspoon salt
- ¼ teaspoon ground cinnamon
- Pinch of baking soda

1. Melt the butter in a medium saucepan over medium heat. Add the sugar, 7 tablespoons of the heavy cream, and the rum, and stir gently with a wooden spoon just to moisten the sugar. Let the mixture come to a simmer without stirring further, then let it cook until it reaches 300 degrees F (use a candy thermometer to be sure). Only stir if you see darker areas forming; try to stir as little as possible.

2. When the mixture reaches 300 degrees F, remove the pot from the heat and very carefully add the remaining 1¼ cups heavy cream (it will create a lot of steam, so wear an oven mitt and stand back). Add the salt, cinnamon, and baking soda, and whisk well to blend. Pour the caramel into a heatproof bowl, and let it cool on the countertop until it's just barely warm, then let it cool completely in the refrigerator before using.

Graham Cracker Crust

MAKES ENOUGH FOR 2 DOZEN CUPCAKES

1 cup plus 2 tablespoons graham cracker crumbs (from about 15 squares)

¼ cup (½ stick) unsalted butter, melted

3 tablespoons sugar

1. Preheat the oven to 325 degrees F. Line two 12-cup muffin pans with cupcake liners.

2. In a small bowl, mix together the graham cracker crumbs, melted butter, and sugar until well blended and no dry crumbs remain.

3. Put 1 tablespoon of the mixture in each cupcake liner. Use the bottom of a small glass to pack the crumbs into the bottom of each liner.

4. Bake the crusts for 5 minutes, then remove the pans from the oven. Let the crusts cool in the pans for 5 minutes before adding the cupcake batter.

Graham Cracker Crust for S'mores Cupcakes

MAKES ENOUGH FOR 2 DOZEN CUPCAKES

1½ cups graham cracker crumbs (from about 20 squares)

5 tablespoons unsalted butter, melted

¼ cup sugar

9 ounces bittersweet chocolate, chopped

1. Preheat the oven to 325 degrees F. Line two 12-cup muffin pans with cupcake liners.

2. In a medium bowl, mix together the graham cracker crumbs, melted butter, and sugar until well blended and no dry crumbs remain.

3. Put 1 tablespoon of the mixture in each cupcake liner. Use the bottom of a small glass to pack the crumbs into the bottom of each liner.

4. Sprinkle 2 teaspoons of the chocolate over each crust (reserve the remaining graham cracker mixture and chocolate for topping the cupcakes).

5. Bake the crusts for 8 minutes, then remove the pans from the oven. Let the crusts cool in the pan for 5 minutes before adding the cupcake batter.

Blueberry Pie Filling

MAKES 1 GENEROUS CUP

- 2½ cups fresh or frozen blueberries
- 4½ tablespoons sugar
- 1 tablespoon lemon zest
- 1 tablespoon unsalted butter
- 1 tablespoon freshly squeezed lemon juice
- 2 teaspoons arrowroot powder or cornstarch

1. Put the blueberries, sugar, lemon zest, and butter in a large pot over medium heat. Bring the mixture to a simmer, stirring constantly so the sugar doesn't burn and crushing the berries as you stir to make juice. Reduce the heat just enough to keep the mixture at a simmer and continue to cook, stirring occasionally, until the blueberry juices begin to concentrate, about 8 minutes.

2. While the berries are cooking, mix the lemon juice and arrowroot powder to make a slurry. When the berries have finished cooking, turn off the heat and then slowly add the slurry, stirring constantly, until the mixture thickens. Cool and use immediately or transfer the mixture to an airtight container and store in the refrigerator for up to 1 week. Bring to room temperature when ready to use.

Candied Rose Petals

MAKES 2 DOZEN

- 1 dozen fragrant miniature roses (unsprayed)
- 1 egg white
- ½ cup superfine sugar

PRO-TIP

If you can't find miniature roses, break down larger petals once they've dried.

1. Remove petals from the roses and pat dry. Choose 24 perfect petals, small enough to be cupcake garnishes.

2. Line a baking sheet with parchment or wax paper.

3. Put the egg white in a small bowl and whisk it until foamy. Place the sugar in another small bowl.

4. Using a pastry brush, completely coat a petal with egg white, then carefully dip it into the sugar to completely cover it. Gently tap off any excess sugar and place the petal on the prepared baking sheet. Repeat with the remaining petals. Let the petals dry in a cool, dry place for 2 to 3 days. Once completely dried, petals can be stored in an airtight container for up to a month.

Caramel Sauce

MAKES ABOUT 1½ CUPS

1⅓ cups sugar

¼ cup cold water

2 tablespoons light corn syrup

¼ teaspoon freshly squeezed lemon juice

2 tablespoons unsalted butter, cut into 8 pieces

1 cup heavy cream, at room temperature

¼ teaspoon vanilla extract

Pinch of salt

1. Put the sugar, water, corn syrup, and lemon juice in a medium saucepan. Stir gently with a wooden spoon just to moisten the sugar. Set the pan over medium-high heat. Watch carefully, but do not stir. The sugar will dissolve and come to a boil; the mixture will gradually turn golden and color to a dark amber (at 320 degrees F, if you have a candy thermometer).

2. While the sugar is cooking, put the butter and heavy cream next to the stove, along with the vanilla and salt. Also have ready a large whisk and an oven mitt. Once the sugar starts changing color, it darkens quickly, so don't walk away. If the caramel is turning darker around the edges, gently swirl the pan, but don't stir. As soon as the caramel is dark amber, remove the pan from the heat and immediately add the butter. Hold the whisk with the oven mitt (to protect your hand and arm from the steam) and stir the butter as it melts. Right away, add the heavy cream in a steady stream, whisking constantly. Be very careful, because the caramel will bubble up and create a lot of steam. Add the vanilla and salt, and pour the sauce into a heatproof container to cool to room temperature. You can store caramel sauce in an airtight container for up to a week in the refrigerator.

ACKNOWLEDGMENTS

This book is a dream come true. All my life, I have loved to make things—beautiful, yummy, crafty things—that make people happy. And my hope is that this book brings happiness and inspiration to all who pick it up.

I'd like to thank Sasquatch Books, especially Gary Luke, for believing in this project, and sticking with it through the long and sometimes challenging process. Special thanks to the uber-creative and talented Callie Meyer for starting this journey with me, contributing so much, and becoming a great friend in the process. I also want to thank everyone on the Trophy Cupcakes team who crafted, baked, and held down the fort while I was utterly consumed by giving birth to this book—especially Nicole Familetti and Antje Kubitz, my power duo.

I raise a glass of bubbly to the incredibly talented women who poured their hearts into this book. I will be forever humbled by the time and energy that each of you put in, all in the name of Trophy. I couldn't have done it without you: Mary LaCoste, Rina Jordan, Jenny Batt, Jenn Elliott Blake, Julia Manchik, Ali Basye, and you, too, Nathan Carrabba. Also: a heartfelt thanks to your families for (mostly) putting up with so many late nights and missed dates.

I'd like to thank Leora Bloom for tirelessly testing recipes to perfection. And a special shout-out to her family: Thank you for being up for the task of eating more cupcakes than seems humanly possible! I'll never forget the line, "Awwww Mom, do we have to have cupcakes again?"

To my beautiful husband and business partner: Thank you for your patience throughout my entire (obsessive at times) creative process. Trophy would not exist without you. And thank you to my amazing son, Fleetwood, for your four-year-old party theme input—you've got the best ideas ever!

Thanks to my mom, sisters, aunts, grandmas, and all of the wonderfully creative women in my family who paved the way for me to follow my dreams, whether you knew you were doing it or not. And to everyone in my family, including the Williamsons, for being movers, shakers, doers, creators, entrepreneurs, and an overall endlessly inspiring bunch.

My heartfelt thanks continue. To Nate Mendel for believing in my wild dream and helping me make it a reality. To Matt Cameron for his rockin' cameo in our Rock Star Party. To Ted Watson of Watson Kennedy for his over-the-top inspiration. To my favorite chef, Matt Dillon, for letting us shoot our Paris Party at his beyond-gorgeous Corson Building. To The Conrad family for letting us take over their beautiful home, twice. To Leslie Margarones and family for being so helpful and enthusiastically cheering on Trophy for all of these years. And a big thanks to all of our friends who were willing to model in exchange for cupcakes!

Last but not least, to my dearest friends Matteo Tacchini, Jessica Ballard, Pandora Andre-Beatty, Sarah Nichols, Jodi Davis, Julie Wray, and Kelley Moore. I would have NEVER been able to open a cupcake shop, grow my business by leaps and bounds, write a book, or any of this craziness without your constant support and unconditional love. I am way beyond lucky to have all of you on my side.

RESOURCES

Most of this book's resources came from Trophy Cupcakes and Party, TrophyCupcakes.com and in Seattle at 1418 27th Ave. 98103, (206) 632-7020; Watson Kennedy Fine Home, WatsonKennedy.com and in Seattle at 1022 First Ave. 98104, (206) 652-8350; and Jenn Elliott Blake, JennElliottBlake.com.

COVER

Royal Icing cake stands at BHLDN.com. **Dot cupcake liners** by Paper Eskimo at TrophyCupcakes.com. **Footed glasses** at CrateAndBarrel.com. **Teacup, plates, and gold spoons** at WatsonKennedy.com. **Straws, striped treat bag, and assorted baking cups** at ShopSweetLulu.com.

Party Planning 101

PHOTO, PAGE 6: **Straws** at ParksidePapers.com and TrophyCupcakes.com. **Spoons, plates, tissue fringe, bakers twine, cupcake liners, and treat bags** at ShopSweetLulu.com. **Doilies** at APartySource.com. **Honeycomb ball** at Devra-Party.com and ShopSweetLulu.com.

PHOTO, PAGE 19: **Honeycomb paper pads** at Devra-Party.com. **Ribbon** at PS-Stores.com. **Crepe paper streamers** at CrepePaperStore.com. **Paper plates** at DisplayCostume.com. **Candles** at CakeDeco.com.

PARTY PANTRY ESSENTIALS, PAGE 18

Crepe paper (wide rolls/Italian) at Cartefini.com, (streamers, folds, and rolls) at CrepePaperStore.com. **Tissue Paper** at PaperMart.com. **Confetti** (tissue confetti) at PartyCity.com, (knot and bow tissue confetti) at ShopSweetLulu.com, (candy confetti) at CandyWarehouse.com, in bulk at CakeDeco.com (under quins, look for "sequins") and in Seattle at Home Cake Decorating Supply Co. **Candles** (my favorite birthday candles) at CaspariOnline.com. **Champagne and wine glasses** (by the dozen) at WorldMarket.com. **Platters and appetizer plates** (by the dozen) at CrateandBarrel.com. **Linen napkins** available at most housewares shops. **Mydrap linen napkins** on a roll at WestElm.com and Amazon.com. **Paper plates and napkins** at CaspariOnline.com. **Ribbon** at MidoriRibbon.com and NashvilleWraps.com. **Paper Straws** at SugarDiva.com, BakeItPretty.com, and TrophyCupcakes.com. **Swizzle Sticks** (rock candy) at OhNuts.com, (vintage) at Ebay.com, (custom) ForYourParty.com, and (plastic) at PartyCity.com. **Vases** at Save-On-Crafts.com and houseware shops like Crate and Barrel, Pottery Barn, and open-to-the-public wholesale florist shops. **Chilling bins/ice buckets** available at most housewares stores.

CRAFT ESSENTIALS, PAGE 20

Scissors at WatsonKennedy.com. **Paper** at PaperMart.com, CreativePapersOnline.com, and Paper-Source.com. **Wrapping paper** at SnowAndGraham.com and RiflePaperCo.com. **Washi tape** at CuteTape.com and most craft stores. **Scissors, glue, etc.** at HobbyLobby.com and most craft stores. **Craft punches** at ImpressRubberStamps.com. **Twine and trims** (bakers twine) at PaperMart.com and NashvilleWraps.com, (pom-pom trim) at MJTrim.com, (rickrack trim) at RibbonJar.com. **Wire and self-healing mats** at HobbyLobby.com. **Glitter** (craft glitter—especially Martha Stewart's sets) at Michaels.com and MarthaStewart.com, (German glass glitter) at Save-On-Crafts.com.

Trophy's Techniques, Tips + Tricks

ESSENTIAL CUPCAKE TOOLS, PAGE 25

KitchenAid Mixer at Williams-Sonoma.com and Macys.com. **Cupcake/muffin pans** (Chicago Metallic) at Webstaurant.com. **Cuisinart** at Macys.com. **Mesh Sieve** (Camford Brand) at SurLaTable.com, and other brands at Webstaurant.com. **Mixing bowls** at Webstaurant.com. **All-Clad mixing bowls** at Macys.com. **Silicone rubber spatulas, kitchen torch, apple corer, whisk, citrus zester, and reamer** at Williams-Sonoma.com, Macys.com, and SurLaTable.com.

TIPS FOR AMAZING CUPCAKES, PAGE 26

Valrhona cocoa powder at ChocoShere.com, WorldWideChocolate.com, and DiLaurenti.com. **Nielsen-Massey pure Madagascar Bourbon Vanilla** at Williams-Sonoma.com. **Cacao Barry French chocolate flakes and Callebaut Chocolate** at WorldWideChocolate.com. **Organic and local produce** at your local farmers' market.

MUST-HAVES FOR YOUR DECORATING PANTRY, PAGE 30

Offset spatula at Webstaurant.com, kitchen shops, and in Seattle at Home Cake Decorating Supply Co. **Wunderbag and pastry tips** at Webstaurant.com and in Seattle at Home Cake Decorating Supply Co. **Portion scoops** at Webstaurant.com and most kitchen shops. **Baking cups** at BakeItPretty.com and FancyFlours.com. **Tints/gel food coloring** (Ateco 12-pack) at Webstaurant.com and in Seattle at Home Cake Decorating Supply Co. **All-natural food tints** at IndiaTree.com.

TOPPINGS GLOSSARY, PAGE 31

Most items listed can be found at FancyFlours.com, BakeItPretty.com, and in bulk at CakeDeco.com, or in Seattle at Home Cake Decorating Supply Co.

PHOTO, PAGES 34-35

Mosser glass cakeplates at TrophyCupcakes.com, WatsonKennedy.com, and Bellacor.com.

Sparkle, Color + Pattern

PHOTO, PAGES 40-41: **Glasses** at WatsonKennedy.com.

SPARKLE: ENGAGEMENT PARTY, PAGE 43

SET THE STAGE: **Clear balloons** at BalloonsFast.com. **Gold glitter** at Save-On-Crafts.com. **Metallic gold striped twine** at ShopSweetLulu.com. **Gold organza table overlays** at SmartyHadAParty.com. **Gold paillettes** at CCartwright.com and MJTrim.com.

PHOTOS, PAGE 44: **Photo booth** at USnaps.com.

GET CRAFTY: **Clear cylinder vases, craft supplies, German glass glitter, traditional gold glitter** at Save-On-Crafts.com. **Millinery flowers** (vintage style) at LubinFlowers.com or (other styles) at Save-On-Crafts.com.

ENTERTAIN THEM: **Flip-book makers** at FlippedOutProductions.com. **Photo booth props** by TheManicMoose at Etsy.com.

PHOTO, PAGE 47: **Flatware and plates** at WestElm.com. **Floral arrangement** at MckenziePowell.com.

SERVE UP BITES & SIPS: **Scout Provisions** at ScoutProvisions.com. **Edible gold dust, gold leaf, and gold glitter** at FancyFlours.com.

COLOR: AQUA POOL PARTY, PAGE 51

SET THE STAGE: **Beach balls** (aqua) at WindyCityNovelties.com or (classic) at BeachBalls.com. **Sunglasses** at OrientalTrading.com. **Pool toys/games** at ToySplash.com. **Slip-and-slide** at ToysRUs.com.

PHOTOS, PAGES 52, 56: **Glasses** at WatsonKennedy.com. **Fiestaware plates and pitcher** at Macys.com. **Ice cream cone holder** at Istawares.com. Wooden spoons at PapercupDesign.com.

SERVE UP BITES & SIPS: **Waring home snow-cone machine** at Williams-Sonoma.com. **Professional snow-cone maker** at Webstaurant.com. **Jic Jac Blue Raspberry soda** at SodaEmporium.com. **Jones Soda Berry Lemonade and custom label sodas** at JonesSoda.com.

GIVE THEM CUPCAKES: **Snow-cone paper cones** at PartyCity.com and in bulk at Webstaurant.com. **Oven-safe rack** (Nifty Cupcake Cone Baking Rack) at BedBathAndBeyond.com. **Nut/Soufflé cups** at BakeItPretty.com for pretty colors and designs, or white ones in bulk at Webstaurant.com.

PATTERN: BABY SHOWER, PAGE 59

PHOTO, PAGE 58: **Plush animals** at LandOfNod.com. **Baby moccasins** at Shop.Freshly-Picked.com.

SET THE STAGE: **Shizen pattern paper** at Handmade-Paper.us.

ENTERTAIN THEM: **Butcher paper rolls** at DiscountSchoolSupply.com. **Disposable paper tablecloths** at CaspariOnline.com. **Crayola fabric pens** at DiscountSchoolSupply.com. **FabricMate permanent superfine fabric markers** at DharmaTrading.com. **Zig posterman paint**

markers at DickBlick.com. **Gerber 4-pack of unisex organic onesies** at Amazon.com. **Clothespins** at OrientalTrading.com.

PHOTO, PAGE 63: **Mini stands** at OhHelloFriend.com. **Gingham spoon** at Sabre.fr.

COLOR: RED PARTY, PAGE 65

SET THE STAGE: **Red crepe paper** (wide rolls) at Cartefini.com.

GIVE THEM CUPCAKES: **Red candy hearts** at BakeItPretty.com or in bulk at CakeDeco.com.

Away We Go!

PHOTO, PAGES 68-69: **Plumeria lei** in Seattle at Hawaiian General Store and Gallery, 258 NE 45th St., 98105, (206) 633-5233. **Vintage maps** at WatsonKennedy.com.

DESTINATION: PARIS PARTY, PAGE 71

SET THE STAGE: **Café lights** at HometownEvolutionInc.com. **Wooden crates** at JoAnn.com. **Wine crates** at WinePine.com, Ebay.com, or search swap meets. **Mini chalkboard signs** at FactoryDirectCraft.com. **Chalkboards** at BillyBoardsMfg.com. **Chalkboard artists** for custom signs by MainStreetChalk on Etsy.com.

PHOTO, PAGES 72-73: Shot at The Corson Building. **Sourdough country loaf** at SitakAndSpruce.com. **Wood and stone cake plates with glass dome and fleur de lis platter** at Anthropolgie.com. **Wood pedestal** at Roost.com.
Various containers at WatsonKennedy.com.
French cheeses, olives, pate, and baguettes at DeLaurenti.com.

GET CRAFTY: **Rit fabric dye** at craft stores and at RitDye.com.

ENTERTAIN THEM: **Pétanque set** at PlayABoule.com. **French flag temporary tattoos** at TattooSales.com (they have over 200 countries!). **Faux mustache stickers** at Etsy.com from various vendors. **Red berets** at Amazon.com. **Putumayo's "Paris" or "French Café" CD** at Putumayo.com.

SERVE UP BITES & SIPS: **Epoisse de Bourgogne, Roquefort, and other French cheeses** (as well as wonderful olives) at DiBruno.com, DeanAndDeluca.com, and DeLaurenti.com. **Natural syrups for French Sodas** (in flavors like elderflower, lavender, French vanilla) at MoninStore.com. **Mustache straws** at Amazon.com, Etsy.com, and TrophyCupcakes.com.

GIVE THEM CUPCAKES: **3-inch biscuit cutters** at MrsCooks.com. **2.5-inch round cutters** at KitchenConservatory.com. **Kitchen torch** at Williams-Sonoma.com.

PHOTO, PAGE 79: **Cake stand** at Anthropologie.com.

DESTINATION: MEXICO, PAGE 81

PHOTO, PAGE 80: **Vintage Mexican plates** from the private collection of Sue Dircks. **Sarape blanket** at ShindigEvents.org and similar at ElChamaco.com. **Papel picado** at Casa Bonampak.

SET THE STAGE: **Oilcloth** at OilClothByTheYard.com or OilCloth.com. **Otomi fabric/textiles** at Stores.Ebay.com/Mexican-Textiles-Museum-Store and JacarandaHome.com. **Serape blankets and party supplies** at ElChamaco.com and Amols.com. **Papel Picado** at CasaBonampak.com. **Papel picado banderitas** (stock and custom) at MexicanSugarSkull.com.

ENTERTAIN THEM: **Sugar skull supplies** at MexicanSugarSkull.com. **Confetti eggs** by MyMercado at Etsy.com.

SERVE UP BITES AND SIPS: **Talavera pottery** at LaFuente.com, TalaveraEmporium.com, and most Mexican markets. **Jarritos** at Amazon.com and most Mexican markets. **Glass beverage dispenser** at CB2.com and PotteryBarn.com. **Glasses** at Anthropologie.com.

GIVE THEM CUPCAKES: **Fleur de sel** at Saltworks.us and most gourmet grocery stores.

DESTINATION: HAWAII, PAGE 88

SET THE STAGE: **Tropical greenery and foliage** at AlohaHawaiianFlowers.com or your local flower market. **Tropical leaf stencils** at TheArtfulStencil.com. **Tropical flowers and leis** at HawaiiFlowerLei.com. **Glass hurricanes, natural sand, and shells** at Save-On-Crafts.com. **Other shells** at SeaShellCity.com.

GET CRAFTY: **Craft punches** at Scrapbook.com and ImpressRubberStamps.com.

PHOTO, PAGE 91: **Vintage wooden pineapple** (similar to shown) at Ebay.com or (new) at HiloHattie.com.

SERVE UP BITES & SIPS: **Koa wood platters** at Ebay.com. **Bamboo plates** at SmartyHadAParty.com, PartyBox.com, and in bulk at Webstaurant.com.

DESTINATION: SEATTLE, PAGE 95

SET THE STAGE: **Space Needle rubber stamp** at ImpressRubberStamps.com. **Plain fabric** at Fabric.com. **Galvanized (French flower) buckets** at WholesaleFlowersAndSupplies.com.

GET CRAFTY: **Seattle Flag image** at Flags-And-Anthems.com. **Bulk coffee filters** at Webstaurant.com.

ENTERTAIN THEM: **Theo chocolate bars** at TheoChocolate.com. **Fran's Chocolates gray salt caramels** at FransChocolates.com. **Top Pot Doughnuts** in Seattle, TopPotDoughnuts.com for locations.

SERVE UP BITES AND SIPS: **Tom Douglas' "Rub with Love"** at Store.TomDouglas.com. **Tim's Cascade Potato Chips** at TimsChips.com and most grocery stores. **Beecher's Handmade Cheese** at Store.BeechersHandmadeCheese.com. **DRY Soda** at DrySoda.com and in stores nationwide.

SEATTLE IN 24 HOURS, PAGE 95: **Watson Kennedy Fine Home**, WatsonKennedy.com. **Susan Wheeler Home**, SusanWheelerHome.com. **Curtis Steiner**, CurtisSteiner.com. **The Walrus and the Carpenter**, TheWalrusBar.com. **Melrose Market**, MelroseMarket.com. **Washington State Ferry System**, WSDOT.Wa.gov/Ferries. **The Olympic Sculpture Park**, SeattleMuseum.org. **Seattle's Great Wheel**, SeattleGreatWheel.com.

Colorful Characters

PHOTO, PAGES 98-99: **Photo booth props** at HeathOriginal.com.

SUPERHERO TRAINING CAMP PARTY, PAGE 101

SET THE STAGE: **Superhero capes, masks, and arm cuffs** at SewPlainJane.com. **Mounting adhesive sheets** (double tack mounting film) at Scrapbook.com.

ENTERTAIN THEM: **Cone obstacles** at OrientalTrading.com.

SERVE UP BITES & SIPS: **Diamond, star, and lightning bolt cookie cutters** at SweetBakingSupply.com. **Plain silver lunch boxes** at Lunchboxes.com. **Gable boxes** at ShopSweetLulu.com or in bulk at PaperMart.com.

GIVE THEM CUPCAKES: **Pop Rocks** at CandyWarehouse.com.

FOREST FAIRY TEA PARTY, PAGE 109

SET THE STAGE: **Mossy runners, mats, rocks, and birds' nests** at Save-On-Crafts.com. **Candy birds' eggs** at CandyWarehouse.com. **Rocks** for crafting and painting at Save-On-Crafts.com or your own backyard. **Edible toadstools** by YourFantasyCake and others on Etsy.com. **Flameless candles** at LampLust.com and most Target stores. **Faux bois shelf liner** (wood grain contact paper) at HardwareStore.com. **Waldorf-style fairy wings** (butterfly wings) by ZiezoDesigns at Etsy.com. **Bamboo plates/utensils** in sets of 8 at AcmePartyBox.com or in bulk at Webstaurant.com.

GET CRAFTY: **Natural willow branches** from 36 to 48 inches at Save-On-Crafts.com. **Yarn** at Yarn.com and BadWomanYarn.com. **Feathers** at PaperMart.com. **Pony beads** at FusionBeads.com.

ENTERTAIN THEM: **Drawstring burlap or jute pouch, glassine bags** at PaperMart.com.

POP ART PARTY, PAGE 115

PHOTO, PAGE 114: **Jackie O print** by Chloe Margarones. **Vintage polaroid** (similar to shown) at RareMediumSeattle.com. **Super 8 Camera** at Ebay.com. **Glasses** at OrientalTrading.com. **Napkins** at Anthropologie.com. **Mosser clear glass cake plates** at TrophyCupcakes.com, WatsonKennedy.com, and Bellacor.com.

SET THE STAGE: **Silver spray paint** at HomeDepot.com and home improvement stores. **Silver balloons** at BalloonsFast.com. **Party glasses** at OrientalTrading.com.

GET CRAFTY: **Tissue paper** at PaperMart.com. **Premade fringe drape or festooning** at BulkPartySupplies.com. **Basic craft supplies** at HobbyLobby.com.

PHOTO, PAGE 117: **Lollipops** (for cocktail) at ThisCharmingCandy.com.

ENTERTAIN THEM: **Warhol-style and other wigs** at VogueWigs.com. **Candy cigarettes** at OldTimeCandy.com. **Super 8 camera** at Etsy.com.

SERVE UP BITES & SIPS: **Rainbow nonparcils** at BakeItPretty.com. **Lollipops** at CandyWarehouse.com and OhNuts.com. **Silver edible glitter** at FancyFlours.com.

GIVE THEM CUPCAKES: **Kitchen torch and apple corer** at Williams-Sonoma.com.

HELLO KITTY PARTY, PAGE 121

SET THE STAGE: **Hello Kitty party supplies** at MeriMeri.com and PartyCity.com. **Hair bows** by JuicyBows on Etsy.com. **Hello Kitty heart sunglasses** at PartyOn7th.com.

GET CRAFTY: **Plain cone hats** at BirthdayExpress.com, PartyOn7th.com, and at DisplayCostume.com. **Pom-poms and rickrack** at FactoryDirectCrafts.com.

ENTERTAIN THEM: **Hello Kitty trinkets** at Sanrio.com.

SERVE UP BITES & SIPS: **Hello Kitty Pasta** at Amazon.com. **Heart and flower shaped cutters** at PartyCity.com. **Pink striped straws** at TheSugarDiva.com and TrophyCupcakes.com. **Hello Kitty serveware** at Sanrio.com.

PHOTO, PAGE 123: **Pink sequin cupcake papers** at Michaels.com. **Red striped spoon** at Sabre.fr.

Fictitious Fêtes

PHOTO, PAGES 124-125: **Vintage film reels and film props** at ShindigEvents.org. **3-D glasses and miniature TV** at McPhee.com. **Party horns** at DisplayCostume.com. **Fiestaware plate and platter** at Macys.com.

BIKE PARADE & PICNIC, PAGE 127

SET THE STAGE: **Picnic blankets** at PicnicWorld.com. **Bamboo plates, forks, and spoons** for 8 at AcmePartyBox.com or in bulk at Webstaurant.com. **Weck containers** at WeckJars.com and WestElm.com. **Tissue paper festooning** at BulkPartySupplies.com. **Crepe paper streamers** at CrepePaperStore.com. **Bike bells and horns** at ChubbysCruisers.com. **Bike tassels** at BeachBikeOutlet.com.

PHOTO, PAGE 128: **Vintage French checked fabric** at RedTicking.com. **Blue gingham Mydrap napkins** at WestElm.com. **Glass, wooden/ceramic berry baskets** at WatsonKennedy.com. **Wooden utensils** at TrophyCupcakes.com.

ENTERTAIN THEM: **Winner award ribbon** pack of 12 at PartyCity.com. **Rosette award ribbons** at AthleticAwards.com.

SERVE UP BITES & SIPS: **Picnic baskets** (new) at PicnicWorld.com or (vintage) at Ebay.com. **Glassine and patterned treat bags** at ShopSweetLulu.com. **Mydrap blue and white check napkins** at Amazon.com. **French blue and white check linens** at Red Ticking.com. **DRY Soda** at DrySoda.com.

PHOTO, PAGE 131: White Mosser glass cake plates at TrophyCupcakes.com and Bellacor.com.

CASABLANCA PARTY, PAGE 133

SET THE STAGE: Moroccan lanterns at HalfPricedDecor.com and WorldMarket.com. **Large plants** rent from a local nursery or party rental shop.

GET CRAFTY: Tissue paper at PaperMart.com. **Corsage pins** at Save-On-Crafts.com.

ENTERTAIN THEM: Custom poker chips at PrintWorld.com and Beau-Coup.com. **Roulette wheels** available at most party rental shops.

GIVE THEM CUPCAKES: Rose water (Cortas 10-ounce bottle) at Amazon.com. EDible rose petals at MarxFoods.com

LIFE AQUATIC PARTY, PAGE 139

PHOTO, PAGE 138: Tolix stools at Design Within Reach. **Cake plate** at RosannaInc.com.

SET THE STAGE: Nautical party props at Save-On-Crafts.com. **Nautical party supplies** at OrientalTrading.com. **Buoys** (inexpensive) at PartySwizzle.com, (vintage-inspired collectors) at NauticalSeason.com, or (vintage) at Ebay.com.

ENTERTAIN THEM: Red knit caps at TheDealRack.com. **Toy submarines and boats, life rings and plastic lobsters, sea horses, and other ocean creatures** at OrientalTrading.com. **Wooden balloon powered boats** at TinToyArcade.com.

SERVE UP BITES & SIPS: Nautical ropes and props, giant resin clam shells at Save-On-Crafts.com. **Nautical tableware** at OrientalTrading.com.

THE VERY HUNGRY CATERPILLAR PARTY, PAGE 145

GET CRAFTY: Tissue Paper at PaperMart.com. **General craft supplies** at HobbyLobby.com.

ENTERTAIN THEM: Popsicle sticks, pipe cleaners, pom-poms, and googly eyes at HobbyLobby.com. **Colorful good bags** at ShopSweetLulu.com. **Eric Carle coloring sheets** at Eric-Carle.com.

GIVE THEM CUPCAKES: Wafer paper leaves at CakeDeco.com.

Pastimes + Passions

PHOTO, PAGES 148-149: Tennis racket charms at McPhee.com.

BAKING: CUPCAKE PARTY, PAGE 151

SET THE STAGE: Bakery and cupcake boxes at ShopSweetLulu.com, BakeItPretty.com, PS-Stores.com, and in Seattle at Home Cake Decorating Supply Co. **Stickers, labels, and tags** at ShopSweetLulu.com. **Kids customizable aprons** at GrowingCooks.com.

GET CRAFTY: Super cute cupcake liners (for garlands and baking) at BakeItPretty.com. **Basic craft supplies** at HobbyLobby.com.

ENTERTAIN THEM: Clear disposable pastry bags at TheBakersKitchen.com and in Seattle at Home Cake Decorating Supply Co.

SERVE UP BITES & SIPS: Nut cups and treat bags at ShopSweetLulu.com and BakeItPretty.com.

MUSIC: ROCK STAR PARTY, PAGE 159

SET THE STAGE: Lanyards and badge holders at 24HourWristbands.com. **Temporary tattoos** (custom) at 24HourTattoo.com and (in-stock) at TattooSales.com. **Custom t-shirts** at MyTrickPony.com. **Custom buttons** at AffordableButtons.com. **Custom embroidered patches** (small quantities) by WoolySpringsCom on Etsy.com or (large quantities) at TheStudio.com. **Rock/music posters** at AllPosters.com. **Rock 'n' roll party supplies** at BulkPartySupplies.com.

PHOTO, PAGE 163: Temporary tattoos at Tattly.com.

GIVE THEM CUPCAKES: Edible silver glitter at FancyFlours.com. **Rock and roll cupcake picks** at Amazon.com. **Rock candy** at CandyCrate.com.

CAMPING PARTY, PAGE 167

SET THE STAGE: **Iconic camping accessories** at most Army Navy Surplus stores. **Pinecones, faux birds, and cross sections of logs/tree stumps** at Save-On-Crafts.com. **Drawstring backpacks** at OrientalTrading.com. **Mason jars** at PeakCandle.com. **Enamelware** at CampingComfortably.com. **Disposable/compostable bamboo dinnerware** at AcmePartyBox.com. **Mini skillets** at Amazon.com.

GET CRAFTY: **Pinecones and twine** at Save-On-Crafts.com. **Bamboo knives** at Webstaurant.com.

PHOTO, PAGE 169: **Toasted coconut marshmallow** at ShopMallow.com. **Wooden berry basket** at WatsonKennedy.com and ShopSweetLulu.com.

SERVE UP BITES & SIPS: **Parchment lined foil** (Martha Wrap Foil and Parchment in One) at Amazon.com. **Vanilla bean marshmallows** by PaperCakeScissors on Etsy.com. **Gourmet marshmallows** at ShopMallow.com. **Green berry baskets** at BakeItPretty.com. **Wooden berry baskets** by WishingCreek on Etsy.com.

BALLERINA BIRTHDAY PARTY, PAGE 173

SET THE STAGE: **Tulle** at PaperMart.com. **Pointe shoes and ballet slippers** at DiscountDance.com.

ENTERTAIN THEM: **Cellophane bags** at PaperMart.com. **Ballet stickers and trinkets** at BallerinaGifts.com. **Ballerina cupcake toppers** at BakeItPretty.com and TrophyCupcakes.com.

PHOTOS, PAGES 175, 176: **Pink Mosser cake plates** at TrophyCupcakes.com, WatsonKennedy.com, and BellaCor.com. **Mini cupcake stands** at BedBathAndBeyond.com.

PHOTO, PAGE 220: **Royal Icing cake stands** at BHLDN.com. **Dot cupcake liners** by Paper Eskimo at TrophyCupcakes.com. **Footed glasses** at CrateAndBarrel.com. **Teacup and gold spoons** at WatsonKennedy.com. **Straws, striped treat bag, and assorted baking cups** at ShopSweetLulu.com.

BACK COVER

Jennifer's dress at KateSpade.com. **Earrings** at CurtisSteiner.com. **Bracelets** at JCrew.com. **Mosser Cake plates** at TrophyCupcakes.com, WatsonKennedy.com, and BellaCor.com. **Dot napkins** at Anthropologie.com. **Paper honeycomb and tissue decorations** at TrophyCupcakes.com, Devra-Party.com, and Distinctive-Decor.com. **Aqua plates** (vintage Coronado Franciscan) at Ebay.com.

INDEX

Note: Photographs are indicated by *italics.*

D

E

F

G

H

I

L

M

N

O

P

R

S

T

ABOUT THE AUTHOR

A life-long baker and party-maker, **JENNIFER SHEA** founded Seattle's Trophy Cupcakes and Party in 2007 with her husband. Trophy was an immediate hit and Jennifer appeared on *The Martha Stewart Show*, cupcakes in tow, in 2008. Her cupcakes have been featured in *Vanity Fair* and *Sunset* magazines, as well as on The Food Network. Trophy now has five bustling Seattle-area locations, and Jennifer was recently named #21 in the "Top Power Players in the Seattle Food World." She lives in Seattle with her family and loves to make every day feel like a party.

About the photographer

RINA JORDAN is a Seattle-based food photographer.